Comedia

NOT the BBC/IBA
The case for community radio

by Simon Partridge

Comedia Publishing Group
9 Poland Street, London W1 3DG. Tel. 01-437 8954

Comedia Publishing Group (formerly Minority Press Group) was set up to investigate and monitor the radical and alternative media in Britain and abroad today. The aim of the project is to provide basic information, investigate problem areas, and to share the experience of those working within the radical media and to encourage debate about its future development. For a list of other titles in the Minority Press Group Series, see page 76.

Simon Partridge has drawn on over a decade of experience of working on the theory and practice of alternative media. He was a founding member of the Community Communications Group, and is active in the Campaign for Press and Broadcasting Freedom.

Acknowledgements

This book could not have been completed without the help of:

Charles Landry, for commissioning it and reviving my enthusiasm when it flagged; Jeremy Scott, for turning my bureaucratese (an occupational hazard if one writes to the Home Office too often!) into more accessible English; Peter Lewis, for providing essential information on North America from his community broadcasting archives; Nicola Crutchley for providing antipodean information; Rachel McCarthy for promptly obtaining Swedish material from the library of the International Institute of Communications; I.S. Uppal, Martin Cumella, Carlos Ordonez and Allan Pond for information on UK experiments; Norman McLeod, for supplying technical information; William Fittall, for keeping me politely informed of the Home Office's non-activity; Joan Munro, for information on the whereabouts of radio workshops/projects; *East End News*, for use of their constitution; Pat Kahn, for efficiently managing design and production under a tight schedule; and last – but by no means least – my colleagues in the Community Radio Group of COMCOM with whom over five years I have sharpened and developed my ideas.

My apologies, in advance, to others in the community radio movement who no doubt deserve a mention – but lack of time, money and mental energy and my share of prejudice, make me aware that what follows is much more the first word on the matter than the last. Finally, to complete the communications cycle, I would be pleased to hear personally from readers – whether in agreement or disagreement (see my address p.63).

Photographs by courtesy of: London Open Radio, p.22; *Morning Telegraph*, Sheffield, p.30; Canadian Broadcasting Corporation, p.50.

First published in 1982 by Comedia Publishing Group
9 Poland Street, London W1V 3DG. Tel: 01-437 8954

© Comedia Publishing Group and Simon Partridge

ISBN 0 906890 18 7 (paperback); 0 906890 17 9 (hardback)

Typeset by Red Lion Setters, London WC1

Printed in Great Britain by
The Russell Press, 45 Gamble Street, Nottingham NG7 4ET (0602 784505)

Trade distribution by

Southern Distribution, Albion Yard, Balfe Street, London N1 (01 837 1460)

Scottish & Northern Distribution, 4th Floor, 18 Granby Row, Manchester M13 (061 228 3903)

Scottish & Northern Distribution, 48a Hamilton Place, Edinburgh EH1 5AX (031 225 4950)

Contents

To my parents and my analyst, and those struggling in the 1st and 3rd worlds to develop participatory, democratically controlled communications systems.

COMMUNICATION VERSUS INFORMATION

The right to inform and be informed implies that the top-down dispensing of knowledge to passive receivers by those who have access to it should give way to a mutually beneficial exchange through sideways interactions, each party being at the same time a provider and receiver of information. This is communication in the proper sense of the term.

Communication should therefore be deprofessionalised to the largest extent possible. All those who feel the need to express themselves should be able to do so without unnecessary professional mediation.

Those who continue to be communication specialists should become aware of this social requirement and their own education should reflect this need.

—From the 'Right to Inform and be Informed' (with necessary translations from international to common English), *Development Dialogue: 1981 no. 2.*
(See Part II section 5 for details)

Part 1: The story so far

CHAPTER 1

A voice for everyone

On the 14th of July 1981 in Parliament the Home Secretary gave the first official recognition to community radio. He acknowledged that he had received many representations calling for such a service and 'proposed to give further consideration to this matter'.

That statement, which received characteristically scant attention in the mass media, expresses an intention whose significance is far reaching.

Though it still remains illegal for anyone outside the BBC* and IBA* (starred items are in the glossary, appendix 1) to broadcast to the general public, for community radio to have won parliamentary recognition represents a very considerable achievement. This success results from four years of hard lobbying instigated by the Community Communications Group (COMCOM),[1] joined more latterly by hospital and student broadcasters, and the experimental cable radio stations.

This official recognition of community radio forms the start-point for this book. In it we shall outline the possibilities of this new service and describe how these may be tested out in practice. We are encouraged by the example of CB* radio, legal since November 1981, and last year's governmental sanction of a pilot scheme for subscription cable TV.[2] We are speaking of what is feasible. The goals suggested are realistic.

The intentions of community radio lie close to the heart of that contemporary desire, shared by so many, for a less centralised, less commercialised but more personal and participatory social order. An open and democratic media is an essential element within the infrastructure of such a state.

This book is not aimed at the technician or only those with experience of broadcasting. We are speaking not just to enthusiasts already engaged in alternative radio such as hospitals, students, CB users and the occasional pirate, but to people whose lives are involved in community action and co-operative development work at a local level. Most importantly we are speaking to those whose experience of radio is in the role of *listener*. Especially to those listeners who feel disappointed or inadequately served, who find the programmes available under the existing systems have little relevance to either their tastes or needs.

Such might well include: many women, trade unionists, blacks, gays and various ethnic/linguistic minorities and special interest groups – e.g. young people and their music, the blind and the housebound – who, given half a chance, might also become broadcasters in their own right.

In the pages which follow we shall explain briefly how broadcasting is now organised and run in the UK, and how it has come to be so. We shall tell how community radio differs in its aims, seeking not to replace or duplicate what exists already but to extend to individuals and communities the benefits of a new and different service.

We will also try to indicate the future of community radio and show what it can mean to you.

The essence of community radio lies in participation. This could be your service, yours not just to listen to but, if you so wish, to organise and to run. The lists are open. The field is a new one. Community radio could be your cause, your hobby, or your job.

NOTES

1. COMCOM was established in February 1977 to lobby for the development of community owned media and information services. It now concentrates exclusively on radio. See Part II section 6, for address.
2. Cable TV originally developed where over-air reception for TV was bad, so that the signal is sent down a cable rather than broadcast. The present experiments are designed to test whether viewers are prepared to pay a 'subscription' to receive non-broadcast programmes – e.g. old films, sporting events, perhaps a little locally originated programming etc.

CHAPTER 2

Existing local radio in the UK – the BBC and IBA

All public radio broadcasting in Britain is provided by the BBC and the IBA.

The BBC is governed by Royal Charter,[1] the IBA by Act of Parliament.[2] Both are controlled by boards composed of members of the public representing the 'Public Interest'. The men and women granted these jobs are chosen by the Home Secretary.[3]

'Independent' in the day-to-day running of their affairs, both organisations are responsible to Parliament through the Home Secretary. It is to him they submit their annual report and accounts. It is he who can remove their licence to broadcast under the Wireless Telegraphy Act.

One may be sceptical of the 'independence' professed by the BBC and IBA. These vital and opinion forming institutions inevitably exist under political and commercial pressures. Both institutions are controlled financially by Parliament, the IBA by a levy upon advertising profit. Their professed 'independence' therefore is not unqualified, and the arguments of professional broadcasters to justify it are often self-serving.

Despite their constitutional obligation to impartiality there is a considerable body of evidence to show that both the BBC and IBA maintain in their management and content of their programmes a persistent bias against the Labour Movement.[4]

Resembling each other in many ways, important differences nevertheless distinguish the two establishments. The BBC is financed out of the TV licence fee, part of which pays for the national radio networks 1, 2, 3 and 4 and the national region networks of Scotland, Wales and Northern Ireland and local radio.

The IBA does not produce its own programmes but awards contracts for this work to commercial TV and radio companies. These programmes are paid for out of the revenue which comes from selling air-time spots to advertisers (in the case of radio 9 minutes in each hour). From this revenue the companies also pay dividends to their shareholders and a rental to the IBA for the use of its transmitters and to cover its administration costs.

It is often claimed by the IBA[5] and its subcontractors that commercial local radio is a 'public service without public expenditure'. The truth is that each of us as a consumer contributes towards the advertising budgets of companies (whether private or state owned) every time we buy goods or services from them. Thus, we all pay for radio and TV financed out of advertising. The only people who can justifiably say they are receiving local radio free are those listening to BBC stations who do not own a television and therefore have not paid a licence fee. The choice is simply whether we pay directly or indirectly, and whether we are exposed to advertisements or are not.

BBC local radio

The British Broadcasting Company (as it then was) – first started broadcasting locally in London, Birmingham and Manchester[6] in 1922, but this early localism was quickly halted and thirty six years had passed before the BBC prepared an overall plan for local broadcasting and began to discuss this with the Post Office.[7] Two years later the Government put the idea to the Pilkington Committee* which had been set up to look into the future of broadcasting. In 1962 this committee recommended the introduction of BBC local radio.

The Government was not prepared to accept the recommendation unless it was convinced that there was a public demand for local radio and it was not until Christmas 1966 that it considered the time was ripe to authorise a two-year experiment to be run by the BBC and comprising nine stations, though only eight were in fact set up. In November 1967 these opened at Leicester, Sheffield and Liverpool, soon after at Nottingham, Stoke-on-Trent, Brighton, Leeds and Durham. In three respects these had important differences from the present day BBC stations: they were largely financed by their respective local authorities; they had Local Broadcasting Councils appointed directly by the Postmaster General (in consultation with the BBC) who were closely involved in policy making on programme schedules, content and finances; and they broadcast only on VHF.*

In August 1969 the Government endorsed the experiment as a success but concluded that local authority financial support was unlikely to sustain a permanent service and local radio would therefore need to be financed out of an increased licence fee. The BBC was given the go-ahead to expand to forty stations and work immediately started on a further twelve.

However, the 1970 General Election brought a Conservative government to power pledged to the introduction of commercial local radio. It issued a White Paper in March 1971 which gave the go-ahead for privately owned radio financed from advertising and which, although confirming the existing twenty BBC stations, halted any further development of them. This remained the position until the Annan Committee had reported in March 1977. The subsequent White Paper on broadcasting published in July 1978 gave the go-ahead for further expansion of BBC and IBA local radio.

At this time the BBC envisaged up to 65 local stations in England and about 30 smaller opt-out* stations in Scotland, Wales and Northern Ireland. But by 1980 the number in England had shrunk to 38 and these new stations were being described as 'county' stations rather than local ones.

They will be on the air for only six hours a day (compared to ten hours for the older local stations), employ around 20 people (compared to up to 50) and cost about £500,000 to set up. It is intended to complete the 38 English county stations by 1987. So far 22 stations are on the air.

Commercial local radio

The event which started local commercial history was more dramatic. It holds a place within the memory of all of us in Britain now aged twenty five or older. Who does not recall the broadcasts of Radio Caroline which opened in March 1964?

The ship-based station was started out of sheer exasperation by a 22-year-old Irish businessman, Ronan O'Rahilly. In 1962 he had recorded a then unknown pop singer called Georgie Fame. He took a recording of Fame around the record companies and got nowhere. He came up against the closed doors of a near monopoly. There were only two large manufacturers, EMI and Decca, and two smaller concerns, Pye and Phillips. Together they accounted for 99% of the market and none of them wanted the record. O'Rahilly's next step was to form his own record company and, somewhat innocently, to take his record to the studios of Radio Luxembourg to ask for air play. There he was shocked to learn that virtually the entire Luxembourg air time was made up by sponsored programmes from the big four record companies. It 'just wasn't possible' for Luxembourg to play another label.

From there he went to the BBC where he was told they only played *established* artists on their one programme a week of popular music. O'Rahilly concluded, logically and boldly, that the only way of getting his record airtime was to start his own station!

Response was overwhelming. Ten days after its opening Radio

Caroline was reported to have received an avalanche of 20,000 fan letters. It was obvious that the 'pirate' station Caroline, broadcasting from outside UK territorial waters with its all-day music format, was a runaway success. Before long many other 'pirates' had sprung up round our coasts, broadcasting illegally into UK radio frequency space but outside the reach of the law.

The Labour Government which was returned to power in 1964 had a slender majority and was unwilling to take decisive action against pirate stations when it knew they had such popular support. It wasn't until a feud between two rival stations resulted in a murder and public scandal, and the appointment of a new Postmaster General firmly opposed to commercial radio in Labour's Government of 1966, that a move was made to close them down. The 'Marine etc. Broadcasting (Offences) Bill' was passed in June 1967 and came into effect on 15 August 1967. Very shortly afterwards all the pirates but Radio Caroline had closed down, and in September the BBC's new four channel service came into operation with Radio 1 as a pop channel.

In time listeners forgot about the past and accepted Radio 1. However, some important changes had taken place as a result of the pirates' actions. They had shown what commercial radio with a mostly-music format financed through advertising could sound like, and it was clear that many people liked what they heard. It forced the BBC to reconsider its programming attitudes and introduce Radio 1 and 2 both modelled on the pirates; and it revolutionised the record industry, introducing many new independent record companies. As a result many new pop groups and singers were discovered who would never otherwise have been heard.

The Conservative Party had been responsible for introducing commercial TV in 1955 and, while they steered clear of officially backing commercial radio when it was illegal, they saw that a similar commercial radio service would be compatible with their sympathy for private enterprise and would at the same time prove electorally popular with many voters, especially the young. It was significant that the forthcoming election was the first in which the 18-21 age group would be allowed to vote.

A Conservative government was duly elected in 1970 and, in line with their election manifesto, published a White paper on commercial radio in March 1971 which required it to offer a 'truly public service' and not be simply a 'vehicle for carrying advertisements'. It was envisaged that there would eventually be a network of up to 60 stations throughout the UK.

The first of these was opened in London in October 1973, the nineteenth in April 1976. Further development was frozen by the

Labour Government returned to power in 1974 pending the report of the Annan Committee, already mentioned.

By early 1982 the IBA had 34 local stations on the air, and intended to increase this by 7 or 8 stations a year leading to a total of 69 stations by 1987. Like the BBC stations, the IBA ones cost on average about £500,000 to set up. The smallest station on air so far has a potential audience of 208,000 and cost £370,000 to launch.

However, doubts are now being expressed as to whether there will be sufficient advertising revenue to support further small stations – since there will be increased competition for listeners among stations themselves (their broadcasting areas often considerably overlap), and there will be competition for the limited advertising revenue from Channel 4 TV (due to start in November 1982) and from breakfast time TV (due to start in May 1983), a peaktime for radio listening.

Other local radio services

There are some other specialised local radio services licensed directly by the Home Office. This is allowed because, strictly speaking, they are not considered to be radio services since they do not use an over-the-air transmitter to distribute their programmes. It is possible that these non-broadcast distribution systems may also be applicable in other situations and we describe them more fully below.

Hospital radio

Hospital radio has been going since 1951. Programmes are distributed via cables from a small studio into the bedside headphones of patients so that only they can hear the programmes. These services are possible because most hospitals in the UK provide some form of bedside radio. Normally this is a relay of the BBC and IBA services, and all a hospital radio need do to broadcast is to plug their own studio output into the system. The services are provided by volunteers, varying in number between one and forty per station.

Programmes cover patients' requests, local news, interviews and sport. Smaller stations tend to concentrate on 'pop' or 'middle-of-the-road' music, but larger ones produce quiz shows, magazines and documentaries. Many groups also undertake programme exchanges.

Equipment varies from being home-made with cheap tape recorders and record decks, to purpose-built studios which may cost upwards of £15,000.

At present there are about 300 hospital radio services broadcasting to about 250,000 patients and serving some 80% of hospitals. Of that number 270 are organised into a national federation, the National Association of Hospital Broadcasting Organisations.[8]

Student radio

The idea for student radio took place around 1967 when some pirate experiments took place, also influenced by the sea-based pop pirates. The first legal broadcast took place at York University in 1969 using induction loop* transmitters.

Potential audiences vary between 800 and 20,000, and setting up costs vary accordingly from less than £5,000 to over £40,000. Running costs are usually between £2,000 and £4,000 a year.

In 1972 student broadcasters came together in the National Association of Student Broadcasting,[9] which now has 23 station members.

The cable radio experiments

Some additional cable radio services were licensed on an experimental basis in 1976. These are dealt with at the end of chapter 4.

In the next chapter we will see how the defining features of community radio have evolved, and how they differ from the comparatively large-scale and expensive BBC and IBA stations we have mentioned.

NOTES

1. This is set out at the back of the annual BBC Handbook.
2. See the IBA Act 1973 and the Broadcasting Act 1980.
3. For further information about this complex but interesting topic see Caroline Heller's *Broadcasting and Accountability*, especially Chapter 3 & 4. In the latter she posits a 'Broadcasting Policy Authority' which would include 'statutory representation of different interests and in certain cases the election of representatives by the interests concerned' – there is no reason in theory why similar procedures should not be applied to the existing broadcasting authorities. Available from BFI Publications, see Part II section 6 for address.
4. See *Bad News* and *More Bad News* by the Glasgow University Media Group, published by Routledge and Kegan Paul.
   Also the TUC have recently published an informative guide for trade unionists (although much of what it says is relevant to any group who feel oppressed by the media). *Critical Viewing and Listening* – available on request from the Press and Information Department, TUC, Great Russell Street, London WC1B 3LS.
5. See IBA Booklet *Independent Local Radio* and the leaflet entitled 'Public Service without Public Expenditure' produced by the Association of Independent

Radio Contractors after the Annan Committee Report was published, encouraging people to write to their MP in support of commercial local radio.
6. For those wishing to pursue the history of the development of broadcasting in more detail the following books will be useful:
   Communications, Raymond Williams
   Television: Technology and Cultural Form, Raymond Williams
   Broadcasting and Accountability, Caroline Heller
   Structures of Television, Nicholas Garnham
   Independent Radio – The Story of Commercial Radio in the United Kingdom, Mike Baron
   The Birth of Broadcasting, Vol. 1 of The History of Broadcasting, Asa Briggs
   See the Bibliography, Appendix 4, for further details.
7. The Post Office was the Government department responsible for broadcasting until 1974, when it was transferred to the Home Office.
8. See Part II section 6 for address.
9. As above.

CHAPTER 3

How the community radio idea developed

The earliest explicit use of the term 'community radio' occurs in Rachel Powell's pamphlet *Possibilities for Local Radio*,[1] in December 1965. However, the idea of highly localised radio services can be traced a good deal further back than this.

The Beveridge Report on the future of broadcasting in January 1951, considering the uses to which the new VHF frequency broadcasting might be put, made this observation:

The scheme for VHF development now in preparation in the BBC is designed first and foremost for this purpose: of completing satisfactory coverage of the United Kingdom by sound broadcasting of the established programmes of the BBC. There is, however, a quite different object, which appears to us equally important – that of making possible a greater diversity and independence of programmes. Use of VHF could make it possible not merely to give the existing BBC programmes to people who now fail to get them, but to establish *local stations with independent programmes of their own*. How large a scope there would be in Britain for local stations broadcasting programmes controlled by Universities or Local Authorities or public service organisations is not known, but *the experiment of setting up some local stations should be tried without delay* . . . There remains for consideration an important problem of authority. Exploitation of higher frequencies in sound broadcasting opens for Britain the possibility of transforming the wavelength situation, and of adding local to centralised broadcasting. It offers this possibility however, only after solution of difficult technical and practical problems. Are we more likely to get full exploration of this possibility by continuing to licence only one broadcasting authority and imposing on it an obligation to develop local broadcasting, or by holding out to entirely independent bodies – a Local Authority, a University or a *specially formed voluntary agency* – the prospect of being able to obtain a licence direct from the Postmaster General? On a balance of consideration we incline in the first instance to try the first alternative, by imposing on the BBC by charter an obligation to develop higher frequency broadcasting particularly with a view to setting up local stations. But *recourse to the second alternative should be kept open*. If a responsible body desired by use of higher frequencies to establish a local broadcasting station for a public purpose with a licence of its own, the Postmaster General should be prepared, after consultation with the BBC, to issue such a licence. *All the necessary conditions securing the nature of the service could be inserted in the licence.*[2] (our emphasis).

The Pilkington Committee report on the future of broadcasting, published in June 1962, recommended that the BBC provide 'local sound broadcasting' on the basis of 'one service in some 250 localities', stations having a typical range of five miles.[3] In its evidence to the Committee the County Councils' Association advocated that 'the way should be left open for the possible future establishment of other stations serving much smaller areas than those covered by the local stations of the BBC and broadcasting during strictly limited hours material of a purely local interest. Such stations would be operated by companies or trusts, in which local authorities would figure prominently, under licence from a statutory authority appointed for the purpose'.[4]

The concept next surfaces in an article published by Richard Hoggart and Stuart Hall in *Peace News* of August 1964 entitled 'Local Radio: Why it must not be Commercial'[5] (Hoggart himself had been a member of the Pilkington Committee). This proposal envisaged a hundred or so stations linked in a loose federation under the BBC.

Rachel Powell's pamphlet, already mentioned, spelt out detailed proposals for up to 250 stations financed partly out of local rates and the BBC's licence fee, again under the loose control of the BBC, although she did not rule out the idea of a separate Trust to administer this new sector of broadcasting. *Anarchy* magazine[6] of November 1968 – prompted partly by the revolutionary events in France earlier in the year which had resulted in a considerable opening up of the highly authoritarian French broadcasting system – devoted the whole issue to 'Radio Freedom', including a lengthy report on non-commercial listeners supported radio in the USA (see next chapter for further details).

The 1971 White Paper (mentioned in the previous chapter) launching commercial local radio produced another crop of counter proposals. We ourselves published a lengthy letter[7] in June 1971 advocating small-scale, non-commercial stations, broadcasting for a limited amount of time a day and financed from a variety of sources including listener subscriptions. Soon after, a group in Cambridge (Cambridge Community Broadcasting) proposed an 'experiment in community broadcasting' and by early 1973 was preparing a non-profit bid for an IBA franchise, but to be financed entirely out of advertising revenue.[8] In the same year a booklet, *Community Radio in Britain – A Practical Guide*,[9] by Nigel Turner

was published. This had drawn upon an earlier pamphlet by David Gardiner which had been part of the first issue of *Undercurrents*.[10] Nigel Turner's booklet put forward the case for 1,000 low power local stations, arguing again from the experience of USA listener financed stations and quoting Brecht on the frontispiece that 'Radio must be changed from a means of distribution to a means of communication'.

By the mid-1970's, aided by the development of cheaper and simpler technologies of production, interest in alternative media and community politics had coalesced into community newspaper,[11] video* and cable TV experiments.[12] It was the imminent publication of the Annan Committee report which brought these interested parties together. As the letter of invitation put it in November 1976:

We the undersigned propose the formation of a COMMUNITY COMM-UNICATIONS group whose aim should be:

1. To lobby for the right of people living in cities, towns, neighbourhoods and other communities to own and/or operate their own television and radio stations.
2. To encourage the growth of communally-owned and/or operated communication resource centres.
3. To promote the continued development of access to and effective participation in national, regional and local broadcasting.

We believe that such a group is essential in the discussion period following publication next year of the report by the Annan Committee, and we feel that the following are likely to be interested in joining:
— the present users of cable networks and potential users of broadcast frequencies for locally controlled and originated radio and television services.
— proponents of public access to resources and decision-making in existing broadcasting organisations.
— groups and individuals working in the field of community communications (whether networked or not).[13]

The Community Communications Group – COMCOM as it soon became known – was formally constituted in February 1977. One of its first tasks was to produce a comprehensive written response[14] to the Annan Report. This it published in June of that year. It strongly endorsed the Local Broadcasting Authority (LBA) proposed by Annan as 'one means of breaking the rigidity of the present duopoly (the BBC and IBA) and of giving local services the chance to develop in a variety of ways' and to 'encourage the growth of co-operative and other joint forms of financing to stimulate a direct involvement by the community in its own broadcasting services'.[15]

In this context COMCOM proposed that 'one of the main objectives of the LBA should be to initiate and encourage the development of a "third force" in British broadcasting. This should consist of highly individual and genuinely local stations. These should be financed from a variety of sources; structured as non-profit-distributing entities; owned and operated by the communities they serve but locally and nationally accountable; openly accessible in terms of production and distribution; and with programming originated locally after thorough and ongoing consultation to identify the needs and interests of the people served'.[16]

Unfortunately, the Labour Government remained deaf to these proposals and merely gave the go-ahead to further expansion of BBC and IBA local stations, although it did encourage the IBA to 'experiment with the Annan Committee's ideas that non-profit trusts should be awarded franchises and that local authorities might be given some role in its local radio stations'.[17]

By 1979 the term 'community radio' had gained general currency and was being widely used and abused by both the BBC and IBA. In order to avoid confusion and diluting the essential principles involved in the concept, in July COMCOM drew up a Community Broadcasting Charter:-

Community Broadcasting should:
 1. serve recognisably local communities and/or communities of interest;
 2. have a non-profit distributing legal form;
 3. have its general management and programming policy made by a Governing Board which is democratically representative of the various interests in the community, including the paid and voluntary broadcasting workers;
 4. provide, within this democratic, non-profit structure, a service of information, education and entertainment, and enable the two-way communication of diverse opinions;
 5. be financed from a variety of sources which could include local loan capital, clearly defined spot advertising of limited duration, and central and local public funds;
 6. recognise the right of paid broadcasting workers to join a union and the need for flexible demarcation of job roles, and allow the use of volunteers where suitable;
 7. undertake to provide equal employment opportunities for women, and for ethnic and other significant social minorities;
 8. be committed to providing local people with access to training, production and transmitting facilities;
 9. transmit programme material that is predominantly locally originated;
10. have a programming policy which encourages the development of a

participatory democracy and which combats racism, sexism and other discriminatory attitudes.

In the light of further experience we would add an explicit commitment to a 'right of reply' in the case of serious misrepresentation, and spell out the grounds of discriminatory attitudes to cover democratic political affiliation and creed.

In August the same year, Aubrey Singer, managing director of BBC Radio, in a speech he gave at the Edinburgh International Radio Festival, envisaged, 'An infinite number of community stations serving 5,000-150,000 people – on air 3-4 hours a day. Advice on the setting up and financing of such stations to be available from the BBC. Money to be raised by the operating community from local sources and stations to be operated co-operatively under licence'.

By the end of 1980 both the Labour Party's Commission of Enquiry and the TUC's Media Working Group had welcomed the 'development towards community radio'. To be joined in 1982 by such well-known figures as Lord Windlesham, formerly managing director of Associated Television[18], and Clive Jenkins and Barrie Sherman of the Association of Scientific Technical and Managerial Staffs.[19]

We can say, finally, that the idea is well and truly born, and in the next chapter we will look at how far it has developed on the ground – or more appropriately over-the-air – both abroad and here.

NOTES

1. *Possibilities for Local Radio*, Rachel Powell, Centre for Contemporary Cultural Studies, Birmingham University, December 1965, p. 19.
2. *Report of the Broadcasting Committee*, Cmnd. 8116, p. 78/79, January 1951.
3. *Report of the Committee on Broadcasting*, Cmnd, 1753, chapter XVII – Sound Broadcasting, p. 221/222, June 1962.
4. *Report of the Committee on Broadcasting*, 1753, Appendix E Vol. II, paper No. 255, p. 1211.
5. Article in *Peace News* of 14 August 1964.
6. *Anarchy* no. 93.
7. *Caernarvon & Denbigh Herald*, 11 June 1971.
8. *New Society*, 25 January 1973.
9. See Appendix 4 for details.
10. 'Community Radio: Practical Advice on the Setting Up of Small Community-based Radio Stations' – published as a separate pamphlet in the first issue of *Undercurrents* the alternative magazine of science and technology, then a do-it-yourself magazine in a plastic bag!
11. See *Here is the Other News*, Minority Press Group, 1980
12. See *Community Television and Cable In Britain*, Peter M. Lewis, BFI Publications, 1978.
13. Letter of invitation to Association of Video Workers, 12 November 1976, signed

by Michael Barrett, Project Director, Channel 40, Milton Keynes; Richard Dunn, Director, Swindon Viewpoint; Derek Jones, ex-North Devon Project; Peter Lewis, ex-Bristol Channel Cable TV; Jekka McVicar, Youth Media Project, Bristol; Rex Pyke, Prodigal Trust, Notting Hill Gate.

14. See *Comments on the Recommendations of the Annan Committee on the Future of Broadcasting*, COMCOM, June 1977.

15. See Annan Committee Report, paras 14.58 and 14.16 respectively.

16. See footnote 14 above, chapter 5, p. 15, para 5.1.

17. *Broadcasting*, Cmnd. 7294, para 39, p. 17.

18. See *Broadcasting in a Free Society*, Blackwell, p. 123-126.

19. See *The Leisure Shock*, Eyre Methuen, p. 157-160.

CHAPTER 4

The idea in practice – abroad and here

In looking at how the idea has worked out in practice, we'll start with some foreign examples since there is now considerable experience of community radio in several overseas countries. It's also worth pointing out that besides the countries mentioned there are developments in Canada, Italy, Belgium, France, and to a lesser extent in Eire, New Zealand, Germany and Spain.

The United States

Community radio began in the USA in 1948 when KPFA, an independent non-profit station supported by listener subscribers many of whom were pacifists and anarchists, started broadcasting from Berkeley, California.

The mid-sixties saw a rapid growth in this type of operation. The National Federation of Community Broadcasters, founded in 1975, now represents some sixty stations.

These early stations shared many characteristics. Each saw itself as a clear alternative to both commercial and public broadcasting,[1] from which they differed in both culture and politics. Their operation was unique in that neither commercial advertisements nor institutional funds paid the bills – the stations instead supported themselves through listener subscriptions, mostly as small as $10 to $15 each.

There was a steady growth in public access and participation. The stations were staffed mainly by volunteers. Opportunities were provided for people to present their views in commentaries, phone-ins, and as programme producers in their own right.

A community station thus came to be defined as a 'non-profit organisation, governed by a board of directors that is generally part community and part station workers (including volunteers)'. Although the Board of Directors has full legal authority for the station, this authority is generally exercised through general policy, budget control, and the employment of key personnel to run the station.

The station staffs in turn generally operate collectively within the Board's guidelines. While all stations have 'general managers', few of these possess executive authority in the traditional sense. Instead, each tends to work as team co-ordinator, the programme organiser, news organiser and chief engineer retaining considerable autonomy in their respective areas. Most stations have few full-time paid staff members – on average about 8 and most of the work is therefore done by volunteers on a part to near full-time basis.

Although financial support comes primarily from the listeners, these subscriptions are supplemented in a number of ways. Many stations sell advertising in their monthly programme guides, and benefit events are common. Some stations receive support from the Corporation for Public Broadcasting, though most do not because of the Corporation's strict criteria on budget size, staffing etc. Other Federal funds will sometimes come from agencies such as those supporting the Arts or job creation schemes. Private foundations and charities occasionally provide donations.

Sources of income for a typical station seem to vary in relation to the length of time they have been on the air. At first, station support comes mainly from listeners and benefits. As the station develops more expertise in fundraising and more visibility the proportion coming from sources such as the Federal government, charities and other grants, tends to rise. A typical breakdown would be: listeners – 45%, benefits, programme guide etc – 25%, federal schemes – 15%, foundations, grants etc – 10%, and 5% from other sources.

The actual size of budgets varies widely, depending on such factors as the size of community served, power of the station, hours on the air etc. There is a critical threshold at which station budgets stabilise – when the rent is paid, running costs are met, there is enough money for some programme purchasing and equipment maintenance plus, of course, a living wage for the full-time staff. Depending on local circumstances this overall sum varies between $70,000 to $105,000.

In programming, stations stress diversity in their music as opposed to the format-bound commercial and high-brow offerings of the public stations (many of which are run by higher education institutions). The stations draw on the music of other countries and explore the USA's heritage of folk, jazz and blues, and generally seek out unheard art forms that extend from the medieval to the avant-garde. The work of local artists is emphasised, often in live broadcasts.

It is in current affairs that community stations most clearly differ from the rest of American broadcasting. There has been a rediscovery of the radio documentary and analyses of local, national and international stories. The stations concentrate on providing alternative viewpoints on the news; uncensored commentary of community spokespersons and live coverage of important events.

Wherever possible community leaders and organisations are encouraged to speak for themselves. Within the limits of the law all are guaranteed access to the airwaves. Remote studios and mobile equipment take the station out into the community to cover meetings, public hearings and cultural events. The access theme is reinforced by the employment of community volunteers and efforts are made to involve and train those normally excluded from the mass media such as women, ethnic minorities, the poor, the elderly and the young.

As Theresa Clifford[2] said to a UNESCO meeting,

At its best, the many elements of community broadcasting come together in a mix of free-flowing and exciting programming. At its worst, it can degenerate into chaos and anarchy or passionately fought disputes among contending groups within the station. We have experienced both extremes.

In general, though, in a growing number of communities, community radio provides an important service to the public that responds to its audience's needs and interests and which is based on a very real sense of participation among a large and diverse group of people working together for a common goal.

Sweden

Sweden initiated a 3 year experiment in 'När' or community radio in the Spring of 1979.

The pilot scheme was deliberately located in 15 widely differing areas, ranging from densely populated sections of major cities to suburbs and rural areas. The aim is to allow local groups to broadcast their own programmes within an area of about 2½ miles radius. Such constituencies include trade unions, political parties, religious organisations, sports clubs, arts and cultural groups, consumer and tenant associations, environmentalists and county colleges – several hundred of these organisations are taking part. The service is non-profit making and no advertisements are allowed.

Organisations can either use the transmitters provided by the National Telecommunications Administration, from whom they will rent on a time-sharing basis (each particular group pays for the time they are on the air), or they can build their own. Access to the transmitter is guaranteed for all groups who maintain at least one broadcast a week.

Groups have to provide their own production studios (though

there is nothing to prevent them sharing these with others), and in some areas Local Authorities have donated a studio.

Närradio does not have to follow the Swedish Broadcasting Corporation (SBC) rules for balance and impartiality, but is subject to the same rules as newspapers. In essence, these allow for expression of editorial opinion (within the law), but provide a right of reply for anyone with opposing views or who has been misrepresented.

Licences to broadcast are granted after formal application to the Community Radio Committee which was established for this purpose by the Swedish Parliament.

In an initial evaluation of the experiment carried out early in 1980 (for which the government has provided a total budget of over £200,000), groups were asked, among other things, why they considered Närradio (NR) was needed in addition to local radio (there are 24 county-wide local stations run by the SBC). 12.6% replied that NR can be given a more personal flavour, and a similar proportion said that NR is better for their organisations than local radio. 9% claimed NR relates better to the local scene. Among the 55% giving other reasons can be found the following: 'We can choose our own time in NR.' 'We want to help break the radio monopoly.' 'NR is better than other media.' 'We escape censorship.'

The following are three examples of NR:-

Järva NR in Stockholm is the most international in Sweden. Thirty groups have received transmission licences. The station transmits in about 10 languages, including Arabic, Icelandic, Finnish and Armenian. Järva NR transmits from four studios, one of which is located in a church.

Jonkoping NR is dominated by church programmes, but the centre of activities is nevertheless the Public High School, where the mass media department produces programmes from its own studio. Two political parties participate, the Liberal Party and the Christian Democrats.

Pitea NR's studio is located in the newly-built municipal library, and the transmitter in the Pitea Hospital. Four political parties participated from the start: Social Democrats, Liberals, Christian Democrats and Workers Communist Party, and there are several other participants including the National Union of Swedish Employers, the city assembly, the Pentacostal Church, and the Merchants' Association.

The experiment will be evaluated in 1982, after which the Swedish Parliament will consider whether there should be a permanent sector of Närradio existing outside of the SBC.

Australia

Community radio in Australia is known as 'public radio' – however, for the sake of consistency we will refer to it as community radio. Despite one or two educational experiments in the early 1970's, the real beginning of Australian community radio stems from the Labour Party go-ahead in September 1974. There are now about 30 such stations in existence and about an equal number in the process of applying for licences. They are grouped nationally into the Public Broadcasting Association of Australia.

There were problems in defining community broadcasting in Australia and these arose partly from the diversity of its origins – and in this respect there may be lessons to learn from their experience. The initiative came from four different sources, and no-one in the early stages envisaged as a goal the system that finally evolved.

The first of these constituents were hi-fi and music enthusiasts who wanted 'classical' music on the airwaves (there being no Australian equivalent of Radio 3). They were of particular importance because they applied pressure both to have the airwaves opened up, and also for the introduction of VHF and better reception. Later joined by 'progressive' music stations, both groups helped establish the idea of minority or special interest stations.

The second lobby was formed by ethnic communities who wanted their own services. Pressure from this constituency caused great confusion and political tension. It was variously proposed that ethnic broadcasting belonged in the national, commercial and public sectors, until, with the creation of the Special Broadcasting Service, it was finally made into a separate sector of its own. However, even after this, ethnic groups were permitted to broadcast over community stations and were granted community licences of their own.

The third group was higher educational institutions, e.g. the University of Adelaide wanted a frequency to extend its adult education courses.

The fourth was composed of more overtly political elements. People argued for the opening up and access to the airwaves on principle. Giving a voice to more people was seen as a way of creating a more participatory and democratic society. The stress here was not on music, ethnic rights or education, but on direct community involvement in broadcasting. Part of this idea was the desire to create a greater diversity of radio programmes from a greater diversity of sources. If one can identify a single unifying concept in Australian community broadcasting, it derives more from these ideas of access and participation than from any other source.

4ZZZ – Brisbane, Australia 6Kw rock, news/current affairs station. Built in 12 weeks by architecture student and 50 volunteers.

Annual budget £65,000. Listener subs £12,000; radiothon £10,000; student union affiliations £15,000; T-shirts etc. £3,000; benefits £25,000.

By 1976 community radio had come to be defined as 'stations operated by non-profit organisations and licensed to serve a geographically defined or special interest section of community'. Community radio was further divided into three categories:

Category E: Licences issued to educational bodies intending to provide programmes of continuing and adult education, but including material designed to enrich the cultural life of the audience.

Category S: Licences issued to groups intending to provide programmes serving a particular interest or group of interests, e.g. music, sport, religion.

Category C: Licences issued to community groups intending to provide programmes serving a particular geographical community.

In 1978, with the new broadcasting legislation finally passed, and the 'experimental' licences of the early stations about to expire, the Australian Broadcasting Tribunal – the body which had been entrusted with the regulation of community broadcasting – embarked on an extensive series of public hearings around the country. 47 applications were received for 26 licences in 15 areas, with considerable competition in the state capital cities. In the event all the existing stations were re-licensed, while 9 entirely new stations came into the system.

Nicola Crutchley, on a fact-finding tour of Australian community radio, had this to say after spending a week at 2XX a Canberra access station: 'After my week-long visit sitting in the studio listening selectively from 6.30am to 1.00am, after watching the queue of people outside the recording studio awaiting their turn to produce programmes at all hours of the day and night, after talking at length to the volunteer workers on the station about radio, after playing flute on a live music show, and after generally getting the feel of 2 Double X, I had one question in my head that refused to go away: Who owns OUR radio waves?'[3]

The United Kingdom

Since only the BBC and IBA are legally allowed to broadcast in the UK, examples that follow are necessarily of a partial or experimental nature. Nonetheless, a survey of community radio, video, and photography carried out by the community arts* newsletter *Another Standard*[4] at the end of 1981 revealed a response 'heavily weighted towards radio' – indicating the large amount of creative energy currently being expended in this field.

Another indicator of considerable activity was the launch in

Autumn 1981 of a quarterly magazine *Relay*[5] specifically devoted to those 'struggling to develop new forms of radio – imaginative, accountable, democratic'. Another is the recent interest shown by at least three of the half-dozen or so CB magazines. *Breaker* even ran its main feature in its February 1982 issue under the title 'Community Radio – The Next Step?' – suggesting some very interesting potential links between CBers and the community radio movement.

Experiments so far fall broadly into two categories: those which are campaigning to set up a community station of their own; and those which have been more content to set up an audio or sound workshop (i.e. a small non-profit recording studio) which produces programmes for distribution on tape/cassette or for access* slots on existing BBC or IBA local stations. Though should appropriate legislation be forthcoming there is every likelihood that such facilities would obtain their own transmitter and start to broadcast.

Gwent Broadcasting Trust

Formed in June 1980, this was the first occasion on which a local community had the opportunity to state its preference for a local station, rather than passively accept what should be imposed on them by the BBC or IBA.

The Trust was born from Gwent Community Radio Steering Group (GCRSG), which came into being as result of a public meeting with wide local support in Newport. The meeting (organised by the Polypill Community Information and Advice Centre with assistance from the Broadcasting Rights & Information Project[6]) was prompted by the decision of the IBA to advertise a franchise for the Newport area. At the same time the BBC had expressed an interest in establishing a small 'opt-out' station from Radio Wales in the area, and it was also known that the Home Office Broadcasting Department was starting to consider community radio stations separate from the BBC and IBA.

At its first meeting at the end of June the GCRSG adopted principles in line with those mentioned in chapter 3. It also set up three research groups:
1. To explore the IBA franchise.
2. To explore some sort of collaboration with the BBC.
3. To search for sources of finance. (The option of setting up a station outside the BBC/IBA was not pursued since it became obvious fairly soon that the Home Office was not going to make any quick decision on the possibility of this being allowed.)

Group 1 concluded that it would be possible to assemble a viable proposal for an IBA station in Gwent and asked GCRSG to produce a 'convincing, realistic and exciting set of proposals for a lively, involving and progressive radio station'. They also sought to establish the station as a non-profit-distributing trust.

Group 2 reported that BBC Wales was keen to establish a small-scale station in Gwent which would probably take the form of a 2 hour per day 'opt-out' from Radio Wales, though 'community access' programmes could be developed over and above this time. The main obstacle to such a development was the BBC's lack of ready cash and there was little likelihood of any progress unless GCRSG could make a substantial contribution to the initial capital cost, estimated at around £125,000 including transmitter. The attraction of a partnership with the BBC was that it would allow for high quality programmes free from commercial pressures. On the other hand the amount of capital needed was considerable, and the audience would be smaller than for an IBA station. It recommended that GCRSG should 'continue to negotiate with the BBC but that this should not deflect us from the pursuit of the IBA franchise'.

At a further meeting to review progress it was decided to pursue the IBA option – while not abandoning the BBC idea completely – and sub-committees were established to examine programme policies, technical aspects including studios and equipment, listener involvement in running a station, and raising finance and establishing a suitable legal structure. A grant of £1,500 was obtained from the Community Projects Foundation and a loan of £3,000 was obtained from Newport Borough Council to help finance the application to the IBA. With this money a local consultant, Joe Miller, was also appointed to be responsible for researching and preparing the application document.

By December considerable work had been completed on programming schedules. The IBA intended to advertise the franchise during the first half of 1981 and it was therefore decided to hold a day conference at the end of January to 'analyse the work so far' and to set in motion one of the following:
— an initiative capable of achieving the IBA franchise for Gwent.
— a proposal to the BBC to develop community radio in Gwent.
— an organisation independent of both the BBC and a future IBA station, but capable of influencing either and of producing community programmes.

From the evidence Joe Miller presented, the conference was forced to face the unwelcome fact that it was impossible to raise the considerable working capital (estimated at £268,000) from non-commercial sources and therefore impossible to establish the station as a non-profit-distributing trust. In the light of this it was decided to withdraw from bidding for the franchise itself and Joe Miller was instructed to bring a company into being in which GCRSG would have two seats on the Board of Directors in exchange for providing 'community' support for the company and donating its research and work to date.

At the same time it was decided to turn the GCRSG into Gwent Broadcasting Trust (GBT) which would have the functions of educating local people in the use of radio and provide production facilities so they could make their own programmes for subsequent access broadcasting. GBT would also seek representation on the board of the company owning the IBA station.

In the event things did not turn out as planned. Gwent Area Broadcasting (GAB), the company set up by Joe Miller refused to reserve places on its board for GBT, claiming that such community involvement would undermine their standing with the IBA. Defeated on this issue, GBT did a deal with a rival bidder, 'Isca Radio', where they obtained seats on the Board.

However, for reasons which remain opaque, the IBA did not award the franchise to Isca, but to GAB. The chairperson of GBT, in a letter to the IBA director of radio, John Thompson, accused it of 'acting against the overwhelming tide of public opinion' in its decision.

Martin Cumella, secretary of GBT, believes that there are several lessons to be drawn from the situation.
— If you enter into an agreement with a second party do so on *your* terms.
— Community support must extend beyond a narrow network of activists and be genuinely rooted in local groups and organisations – and as Gwent proved, it is dangerous to hand over complete control to any one individual.
— Whilst it is essential to work out a structure for democratic management and policy-making, it is equally important to devote attention to the nature of programmes to be broadcast.

On the face of it GBT may sound depressing but their future is not entirely bleak. They are setting up their own radio workshop in conjunction with Community Service Volunteers,[7] and the BBC have agreed to transmit suitable programmes either nationally, over Radio Wales, or on the opt-out stations planned for Newport and the Heads of the Valleys.

The moral of this story seems to be 'keep on trying'. And how different things might have been if a community radio licence had been available!

Hounslow Community Radio

Hounslow Community Radio is a project that has grown out of an initiative taken by the Hounslow Community Relations Council, in particular, Mr Uppal the Senior Community Relations Officer. He sees existing mainstream broadcasting as 'not catering adequately for local needs . . . in an area which is suffering from a period of substantial communication difficulties and cultural adjustments due to the significant change in the racial composition over the last few years'. (It is worth noting in this context that the three existing 'local' stations in London serve upwards of 10 million potential listeners.)

He intends the station should promote good community relations in the area, help develop its variety of cultural and artistic traditions, and provide a service of information about local government and educational, health and community services, in both English and the main ethnic languages. A special aim of the project would be to help members of the ethnic minorities to acquire the social skills needed to make the best use of local agencies and social services. He envisages the project being run by a management committee which would represent the Borough Council and all the main sections of the community, but under the auspices of the Community Relations Council.

A feasibility study envisages capital being raised from membership shares of nominal value (as happens in many of the new co-operatives), central government or its agencies (e.g. the Commission for Racial Equality which funded the feasibility study), local government, grants from charitable foundations, private and commercial donations. Running costs were seen as coming from annual listener subscriptions, central and local government, sale of advertising, merchandising, hiring out of studio facilities, promoting local concerts, fund raising events etc.

Although it was recognised that programming could only be finalised after very close consultation with the local community, it was envisaged that it would cover such things as: amateur music, drama and poetry; discussions, political forums and religious affairs. There would also be phone-ins, in particular to local councillors; platforms for MPs, the police and social services; and 'What's On' announcements and promotional information about such things as the Community Relations Council's mobile information unit, public libraries and emergency opening hours of chemists etc. Also recognised was that with a general emphasis on 'access to the airwaves' particularly for the ethnic minorities in the area, quite unexpected interests would appear and be catered for. When not broadcasting its own programmes the station might opt-into* one or other of the existing London stations.

The technical section of the study included detailed plans[8] for studios specially designed for non-professionals and potential sites for medium-wave and VHF transmitters. Studio equipment and installations were costed at between £39-51,000, depending on how much labour was donated and the sort of premises available. Transmitters[9] were estimated to cost a further £6,000-7,800 to buy and install.

Staffing was envisaged as being a station co-ordinator/news editor; a community liaison worker responsible for explaining and promoting the activities of the station, and organising programme workshops for volunteers; an engineer-cum-presenter responsible for maintaining the technical equipment; and an administrator responsible for secretarial services and admin. support to workers and volunteers.

On the basis of the feasibility study and widespread support Mr. Uppal has applied to the Home Office for an experimental licence. As with other applicants the outcome depends on Home Secretary's forthcoming deliberations (see next chapter).

RADIO WORKSHOPS

There are now several of these scattered around the country[10] and we will take a look at a couple of them.

Islington Radio Project

Islington Radio Project is based at a recording studio attached to the Islington Bus Co. – which belying its name is actually a community arts group. The project was set up in October 1980, but has been hampered by a lack of continuity in its funding which has so far come from the community arts panel of the Greater London Arts Association with lesser assistance from the Inner London Education Authority.

The project development worker Carlos Ordonez, is keen to explore new ways of using low-cost radio technology and sees his initial work as 'very much being in a developmental and experimental phase', and hopes that his funding bodies will not be too impatient for results. The project has already provided the base for a number of initiatives.

African Dawn a group of musicians and poets have made a programme of their work which at the same time explains how they set about things. Friends of the Earth made a programme around a debate on nuclear issues recorded locally and intended for distribution on cassette. In the Spring of 1981 the Alternative Talking

Newspapers Collective Project was launched to provide the blind and partially-sighted with readings of articles, news items and events from a range of radical publications, and will include a feminist edition.

Carlos is also working to establish an Islington Radio News Service, run by a collective of local groups which would produce a regular cassette with local news items, commentary, features, diary of events, interviews and platforms for different viewpoints.

The radio project would distribute the cassettes and local resource centres would supply playback machines. Subscribers would pay a deposit and postage, returning the cassette by a certain date to be rerecorded, and enclosing a feedback/suggestion slip. Open editorial meetings would decide on content of the next edition, evaluate any suggestions and allocate work.

Carlos sees the news service as 'providing groups with an opportunity to explore the issues of news production, questions about "balance", and at the same time establishing a local sound archive'. One impetus behind the service is the lack of an effective distribution system for existing programmes, and he thinks it would be much easier to get things under way 'with an over-air broadcasting outlet'.

Commonsound

Commonsound is a radio workshop in Sheffield. Established in Autumn 1981, it forms part of the Commonground Resources Centre which provides facilities such as a photographic darkroom, litho and silk screen printing, meeting rooms, play area, creche and cafe, for use by the local community.

The centre is run as a self-managing collective. Decisions are taken at fortnightly meetings composed of two representatives from each branch of the operation. Membership of the centre is available to everyone willing to help in its running and meetings are open to all.

Two full-time and three part-time workers are paid by means of grants from Yorkshire Arts Association and the Rowntree Charitable Trust. However these do not cover overheads which amount to roughly £5,000 a year and are met from members' donations paid by standing bankers order.

The studio is now fully operational – complete with Uher portable recorders and reel-to-reel tape machines – and production in full swing, with the workshop hard-pressed to keep up with demand.

'The studio exists for people in the community to make tapes for local radio or tape/slide shows or to get involved in talking

Commonsound in action: Allan Pond (with headphones), Mike Flint (seated), and Chris Meade.

newspapers,' says Chris Meade, the workshop worker. 'The idea is for people to gain the technical knowledge necessary to be able to use the media. We're taking the mythology out.'

In the operation's short life a number of projects have been successfully completed. Commonsound has produced programmes on nuclear disarmament, reggae, black culture, sexual politics and a summer play scheme.

Projects in preparation include a documentary about the mass trespasses on the Yorkshire moors in the 1920's and 30's, and a compilation of local ex-servicepeople's reminiscences of World War II. The workshop has a weekly 10 minute access slot on BBC Radio Sheffield which it hopes to extend.

THE CABLE RADIO EXPERIMENTS

The cable radio experiments – although strictly speaking not considered legally to be radio broadcasting since they distribute their programmes down a cable rather than over-air – are worth a mention for the cautionary lessons we might learn more than anything else.

The experiments grew out of an initiative taken by the Telford Development Corporation (responsible for the new town) in 1975. They commissioned a former producer of the Bristol Channel community cable TV station to produce a feasibility study for a similar service in Telford, but operating on sound only. It was largely in response to this that the Home Office announced in August 1976 that it would allow some experiments subject to the following conditions:-

— programmes must be specifically designed to appeal to the local community and must not contain more than a small proportion of commercially recorded music;

— applicants must satisfy the Home Office that programme standards are acceptable and will be required to pay a licence fee sufficient to cover Home Office expenses in granting the licence and supervising the experiments;

— no sponsored programme will be allowed and applicants will have to show that they can obtain sufficient finance for the service they propose to provide;

— applicants will be required to enter into early consultations with the local communities as to the operation of the experimental services.[11]

Stations were subsequently established at *Basildon, Greenwich*, Milton Keynes, Newton Aycliffe, Swindon Viewpoint (alongside its cable TV operation), *Thamesmead* and Telford itself. At the moment only the italicised[12] are operational, the remainder having closed for economic reasons.

All the stations had a non-profit-distributing financial status and were financed out of a mixture of grants and advertising. However, it was as the grants were progressively withdrawn that the revenue from advertising proved insufficient to bridge the gap – there was also increasing competition from new IBA commercial stations. But apart from Telford and Swindon Viewpoint, none had a democratically elected governing structure – and in all cases those elected/appointed had to be approved by the Home Office.

A recent questionnaire we circulated to the cable stations revealed that all are now heavily dependent on 'commercially recorded music' for their programming. A systematic study of

Aycliffe Community Radio[13] at the end of 1979 revealed that on average 44% of transmission time was given over to records in comparison to 0.7% for locally recorded music, and a further 12.7% was filled by commercially pre-recorded tapes (COI[14] fillers produced on behalf of organisations like the Canned Foods Advisory Service and some commercial firms). Such a proportion would appear to be considerably larger than the 'small proportion' indicated in the original Home Office conditions.

The third report of the Home Office Local Radio Working Party* had this to say about the experiments: 'In the absence of firm evidence there is clearly room for differences of opinion, and it is probable that the extent of public support for community radio, or for different kinds of it, could only be established in the light of further experience not limited to cable.'

One reason why only limited conclusions could be drawn was that distribution down a cable severely hampers reception of programmes – you have to be attached to the cable and a portable set is not practicable. The other is that the Home Office initiated the experiment without either organising or insisting on adequate research to measure the result – in stark contrast to the Swedish Närradio experiments. If over-air community experiments do receive sanction it is vital that a properly organised research programme is set up at the same time to evaluate results.

NOTES

1. The federally funded alternative to commercial broadcasting established via the Corporation for Public Broadcasting.
2. She gave this report representing the National Federation of Community Broadcasters to a meeting on 'Self-management, Access and Participation in Communications' at Belgrade in October 1977.
3. Nicola Crutchley is broadcasting liaison officer of the New Zealand Council of Adult Education, see her article 'Community Radio in Australia', *Continuing Education in New Zealand*, Vol. 2 No. 1, p.86/87.
4. Community Communications issue, Jan/Feb 1982, *Another Standard* (see Part II section 5 for address).
5. *Relay* Issue No. 2 March 1982 includes articles on: community stations in Australia and America; student radio; women's groups making programmes in Sunderland, Cardiff and Southampton; Part II of the True History of Broadcasting in cartoons; CB's potential. See Part II section 5 for address and sub. details.
6. The Broadcasting Rights & Information Project was established by the author in May 1979 for 14 months with a grant from the Calouste Gulbenkian Foundation, to provide help for communtiy-based IBA radio franchise applicants and, latterly, community radio initiatives.
7. Community Service Volunteers runs a media development office which encourages voluntary organisations to make better use of local media, particularly local radio. See Part II section 6 for address.

8. See Part II section 3 for details.
9. As above for details.
10. See Part II section 4 for addresses.
11. Hansard, 4 August 1976, p.792.
12. See Part II section 4 for addresses.
13. *Aycliffe Community Radio – A Research Evaluation*, Robin McCron and Jo Dungey, University of Leicester, Centre for Mass Communication Research, June 1980.
14. The Central Office of Information is the government's official information service.

CHAPTER 5

The next steps and your part in them

As should have become clear whether community radio has any future depends upon government authorisation. In this chapter we'll look at where we've got to, a little at how we got there, and what we must do next to achieve this.

The Home Office attitude to community radio

In April 1978 COMCOM proposed to the Select Committee on Nationalised Industries then investigating the IBA 'a new sector of autonomous non-profit, community-based local radio – one which is *not* mainly dependent on advertising'.[1] Reacting to this submission, the Committee recommended that 'future plans for broadcasting in the UK should encompass the possibility of frequency assignments to provide very low-power transmission facilities for voluntary community radio services within small communities'.

This recommendation was taken up by the Home Office which undertook to 'examine in due course the scope for low power services within the context of plans for the development of local radio as a whole'.[2] In turn it gave rise to part II of the Third Report of the Home Office Local Radio Working Party (HOLRWP) which sought to establish 'what type (or types) of community radio its advocates would like to see, what they believe it has to offer, and the implications of some form of development of community radio in terms not only of frequencies, but of other important and relevant matters, such as the implications for existing broadcasting policy, programme standards, finance and the question of a suitable regulatory structure and the resources that would be involved in regulation'.

The report admitted that the real demand for community radio could only be established in the light of further experience not limited to cable transmission. As regards regulation of community radio services, it cited the long-established principle that 'broadcasting services should be provided only as public services and only by public authorities specifically set up for the purpose, whose governing bodies are appointed as trustees of the public interest in broadcasting and are accountable through the responsible minister to Parliament'. It also quoted the Annan Committee, that these arrangements 'do not admit that anyone with a claim to broadcast has a right to broadcast'.

The HOLRWP report identified five areas which needed detailed scrutiny:-

a) the objectives of community radio services;
b) programme standards;
c) who should be authorised, and by whom, to provide community radio services;
d) supervision and control arrangements;
e) technical matters.

As regards objectives, the report implied a lack of agreed objectives for community radio, thus ignoring aim 4 of COMCOM's Community Broadcasting Charter which calls for a 'service of information, education and entertainment, and (to) enable the two-way communication of diverse opinions', and disregarded the similar objectives stated in the Association of Community Broadcasting Stations'[3] code of practice. However, it did go on to say that objectives were important because 'they imply that the justification for the services is that they would serve the interests of their respective local communities and not simply the tastes and interests of those who would like to broadcast'.

Moving on, it noted that point b) was crucial since the 'nature of programme standards would have a significant bearing on the appropriate regulatory regime for community radio and the resources which that regime would require'. It did not have any detailed suggestions about standards, but indicated a range of possibilities from those already applying to the BBC and IBA, to leaving operators free to broadcast what they liked subject only to the law of the land and such self-regulation in the form of codes of conduct as they chose to subscribe to.

On 'authorisation' it commented on the potential problems of several applicants competing for a licence, and questioned whether schemes should be authorised on a first-come-first-served basis or should there be time-sharing arrangements or other criteria applied such as evidence of community support.

As regards supervision and control, three possibilities were considered:

1. A Community Broadcasting Authority similar to the IBA with the 'specific function of encouraging and regulating the development of community radio'. However, the rejection of the Local Broadcasting Authority (a recommendation of the

Annan Committee), and the current economic climate were
seen to act against this development.
2. The BBC and IBA were considered as candidates, but both were
seen to be fully committed in carrying out the expansion of their
own services for the next few years.
3. The Home Secretary was discussed as a possibility but rejected
on the grounds of constitutional precedent – i.e. 'broadcasters
should be independent of (amongst others) the Government of
the day' – and also because the Home Office was unlikely to
have the resources to undertake any additional supervisory responsibilities.

On 'technical matters', it was noted that 'the issue of a licence to
broadcast is a function conferred on the Home Secretary by legislation'. It followed that he would also have to be responsible for
determining the technical standards of community radio, although
it accepted that the supervision of such standards could be delegated
to another body, perhaps the licensing authority.

As to finance, it was considered that community radio should be
'self-supporting' – in its running costs and cost of supervisory
arrangements.

The report concluded by examining the possibility of an experiment in community radio but was sceptical on two grounds. Firstly, it
claimed that a 'much clearer view than exists at present that community radio (or particular kinds of it) ought to be allowed to develop in
the next few years, together with some consensus about the regulatory
framework which might be applied which the experiments should be
designed to test'. Secondly, it saw such experiments as requiring a fair
amount of resources to evaluate and monitor and doubted whether
the Home Office would have the wherewithall to do this.

It ended by saying, 'the opportunities for community radio
might be followed up at an appropriate time, and we remain of an
open mind on this subject'.

The community radio movement's response

The lukewarm tone of the report and the recommendation of delay
in the seeming hope that the whole tiresome problem would go away
prompted a lively response.

The Home Secretary had asked for comments. At the end of
April 1981 he received an open letter[4] from a widely-based coalition
of community radio supporters representing hospital and student
broadcasters, cable radio stations and many other groups as well as
COMCOM.

Vigorously argued, the letter described community radio as a 'natural development from the present system of public service broadcasting ... bringing increased public participation, accessibility and accountability'. It claimed 'the laws of the land' were sufficient protection against abuse of freedom of the airwaves, but added that 'community radio should be wholly owned and operated by the communities it serves through broadly representative non-profit-distributing bodies financed from a variety of sources'.

It urged the Home Secretary boldly to stimulate this form of broadcasting and proposed he:

— authorise *now* a pilot scheme for community radio, making frequencies and broadcasting licences available to community stations;
— set up a new body to assist in establishing and monitoring the pilot schemes and to examine the long-term potential of community radio and to make recommendations about future policies towards it.

The open letter made a number of criticisms of the Home Office report and the distortion of facts which it contained. In particular the writers questioned its conclusion that 'the demand for community radio in the UK comes essentially from those who want to broadcast rather than the public'. They asked if there was any community in the UK which had been asked whether it wanted a local radio station and, if so, how it wanted this controlled.

The letter criticised the present system of planning local radio as being 'too Whitehall-based' and indifferent to the views and tastes of the communities it is supposed to serve. It went on to protest at the way in which HOLRWP had published their report before seeking the public's comment, and that no public hearings had taken place in the community before decisions were imposed.

The letter noted with approval the report's observation that 'the existing cable sound experiments appear to have secured good local support' (this was before the financial crises mentioned) but regretted that it failed to draw the obvious conclusion that those areas which had proved a demand for community stations should get them. Instead it noted that the report slid into a specious discussion of the need to show 'demand for community radio in the UK as a whole'.

The writers submitted that these inadequacies demonstrated the need for a completely new initiative and a community radio experimental pilot scheme. In order to bring this about they urged the immediate setting up of a Community Radio Working Party (CRWP) to examine the potential and assist in establishing and monitoring such a scheme. They proposed that this should consist of ten people, half of whom would represent community radio interests, and the other half representatives of the Home Office, appropriate government departments and the general public.

As regards the pilot scheme the CRWP would:-
— advise interested groups on how to apply for frequencies;[5]
— advise the Home Office when requested on which groups should be granted frequencies under the scheme, should there be a conflict between applicant groups;[6]
— monitor the stations licensed under the scheme.

As regards future developments the CRWP should also:
— consider what general structure, system or 'regulatory framework' would enable variety to flourish in community radio;
— monitor the different systems of accountability operating in community radio stations and consider other alternatives;
— consider how best to allocate frequencies to community radio;
— consider how best to establish citizens' right of access to the microphone and right of reply;
— consider how community radio can be funded;
— consider how community radio stations should be licensed following the ending of the pilot scheme.

The CRWP was also to be empowered to take evidence from interested parties of all sorts, including the BBC and IBA; cable, hospital and student stations; local communities throughout the country; and any other relevant groups or individuals.

The CRWP was asked to make two reports: an interim report on the early development of the pilot scheme and the stations licensed under it, and a second report early in 1983 making recommendations on the development of community radio in 1984 and beyond.

As we said at the start of chapter 1 this spirited response and detailed counter-proposals did wring an official recognition from the Home Secretary, and the promise to look further into the matter.

However, further probings of the Home Office prior to this booklet going to press (March 1982) revealed a continuing, if polite, dithering on their part (see letter p.39). This was 'explained' by the fact that they had been too busy dealing with direct satellite broadcasting[7] and the expansion of cable TV systems – though we *are* now assured that the topic is finally under active consideration.

A decision is promised within months rather than weeks, though there is no guarantee the answer will be 'Yes'. And there are hints that the current financial problems of the smaller IBA stations may count against the establishment of a 'third force' on the grounds that it would provide unwelcome competition – though why this should bother a Tory government dedicated to lakerism* is hard to see.

HOME OFFICE
Queen Anne's Gate London SW1H 9AT

Mr Simon Partridge
COMCOM
92 Huddleston Road
LONDON N7 0EG

Direct line 01-213 4230
Switchboard 01-213 3000

Your reference

Our reference

Date 20 January 1982

Dear Mr Partridge

Thank you for the documents which I received this
morning. I have managed to have only a quick look
through them so far but I hope to be able to read
them more thoroughly within the next few days.

Yours sincerely

W R FITTALL

Thanks, but where's the action?

For years the proponents of CB radio were met by the same indifference, evasiveness and bureaucratic apathy – one might even call it the use of procrastination as an instrument of government. Only when more than 250,000 CB radios were actually broadcasting on Britain's roads was Parliament obliged to legalise their use and the Home Office to license them.

The lesson to be drawn from this, and the earlier sea-based pop pirates, is that the Home Office has proved to be singularly incapable (so far) of initiating new developments in broadcasting without considerable and consistent pressure from the outside, much of which has been extra-legal. Success for the third force seems assured only if we can maintain sufficient unity of purpose, effort and individual and group willpower.

And if the Home Office fails to move in this direction quickly enough we can surely expect the radio 'Jolly Rogers' of the present few (mostly London-based) Sunday afternoon enthusiasts, to be joined by increasing numbers of those explicitly committed to a new, participatory version of 'public service' radio.

If you feel like joining in – and we hope you will – the first thing to do is write a letter in support of the campaign to the Home Secretary[8] and your MP. Then turn to Part II for further ideas . . .

NOTES

1. Tenth Report from the Select Committee on Nationalised Industries, IBA, Vol II, p.125, HMSO no. 637-II, July 1978.
2. Observations by the Home Secretary and the IBA on the Tenth Report (above), p. 6, HMSO Cmnd. 7791, December 1979.
3. The Association of Community Broadcasting Stations represented the cable radio experiments.
4. Copies of the open letter are available from COMCOM Publications, see Part II section 5 for details.
5. See Appendix 2 for the open letter's detailed suggestions.
6. As above see Appendix 3.
7. On 5 March 1982 the Home Secretary announced that direct satellite broadcasting would start in 1986, initially with the BBC being responsible for two channels. One, called Window on the World, will offer a mix of programmes from abroad and repeats from BBC-1 and -2, and would be financed from a supplementary licence on receiving equipment. The other would be a subscription channel consisting of feature films (shown within weeks of release), concerts, operas, drama and sporting events now shown only in part.
8. The Home Secretary's address is: 50 Queen Anne's Gate, London SW1H 9AT. Your MP can of course be reached at The House of Commons, London SW1 0AA.

Part II: Things to help you on your way

SECTION 1

Getting a community station off the ground

Getting a station started will require a number of steps if it is to be assured of widely-based community support. These steps will be something along the following lines.

The initiators draw up a preliminary outline for a community station drawing on outside advice and others' previous experience where necessary. This preliminary proposal is then well-publicised through letters to voluntary organisations, religious groups, trades unions, professional bodies etc; news releases to existing local media; personal contacts, public meetings etc. – to see if there is sufficient support to develop the idea further. If there is, a Steering Committee is formed with powers of co-option to work up the idea and report its recommendations for general approval several weeks hence.

The Steering Committee establishes several sub-committees to examine such topics as:
— suitable constitution and legal form;
— costs and fund raising;
— programmes and staffing;
— technical aspects of studios, transmitter and premises.
It will also have to decide whether or not to employ a full- or part-time worker to co-ordinate this work.

This work results in the production of a 'licence application document' which, once approved by a public meeting, is then submitted to the Home Office Broadcasting Department (see note 7, chapter 5 for address) for the issuing of a 'pilot community radio licence'.

If the application is approved a broadly representative Committee of Management is formed (see next section for suggestions on management structure). The Committee then proceeds to hire the station manager and to set in train the construction of studios and transmitter, detailed planning of programmes and programme workshops for volunteers, hiring additional staff, promoting the station's existence etc.

A possible democratic structure for a community station

Although there is probably no one blue-print which will satisfy the particular needs of different local communities, the following is intended as a possible general model which could be adapted to local needs. It seeks to embody a major principle of community radio in which both the listeners and the producers (whether full-time or volunteers) should have a say in running the station. At the same time it caters for reasonable operational efficiency and clear lines of legal responsibility.

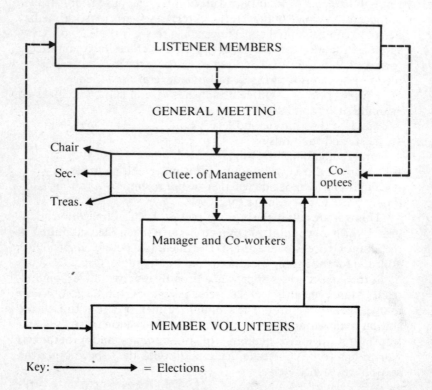

Key: ⟶ = Elections

Above is a schematic model based partly on the example of the East
End News Co-operative, which was established to run a democratic,
non-commercial local newspaper in the East End of London in
April 1981. The functions of the constituent parts are as follows:-

General Meeting
— Makes general station policy
— Elects part of the Committee of Management representing the
  listeners
— Audits the accounts at the AGM.

Committee of Management
— Appoints general manager and full-time workers
— Arbitrates in disputes between station workers and listeners
— Keeps a watching eye on station policy between general meetings

Manager and Co-workers
— Day-to-day management of the station
— Programme production, particularly topical news and informa-
  tion
— Technical maintenance
— Training volunteers
— Elect minority to Committee of Management

Member Volunteers
— Enable the greatest possible degree of member participation in
  the station by helping in the organisation and making programmes
— Might also elect representatives to Committee of Management

Co-optees
— Appointed by elected members of the Committee of Management to represent important minorities – e.g. ethnic, disabled
  etc. – who might not otherwise get represented

Examples from a constitution

What follows are extracts from the constitution of the *East End
News* which could easily be adapted for a radio station. The numbers refer to the paragraphs of the constitution.

2. *Objects* – The objects of the society shall be the publication of a local
newspaper in East London and providing member organisations with assistance in the production of their own bulletins and newsletters.
5. *Membership* – The society shall consist of the founding members

together with such persons or societies as shall hold not less than the minimum number of shares as required by the rules, and as may be admitted to membership by the committee.

14. *Value of Shares* – The value of the shares of the society shall be the nominal value of £1. Each member shall hold at least five shares, and no member (other than a society) may hold more than £5,000 in shares.

15. *Payment for Shares* – In the case of members who are not employees, shares shall be paid for by direct contribution, and in the case of employee members, shares may be paid for either by direct contribution or by allocation of bonus earnings or share of profits as provided hereafter.

16. *Description of Shares* – Shares shall be transferable, and withdrawable but only at the discretion of the Committee of Management.

18. *Power to Obtain Loans* – The society may upon terms and conditions as the Committee think fit obtain loans from time to time for the purposes of the society and mortgage any of its property and issue debentures and other securities. Provided that the amount of money advanced for the time being remaining undischarged, excluding bank overdraft, shall not at any time exceed twice the then nominal capital of the society. The rate of interest on advances shall be determined by the Committee, subject however, to a limit in respect of advances (other than bank overdraft) of 1% above the Bank of England's Minimum Lending Rate, or 5%, whichever is the higher.

35. *Meetings* – Meetings of the society shall be either ordinary meetings, or special meetings. Every member who under these rules has a vote shall be entitled to attend such meetings on the production of such evidence as the Committee may from time to time determine.

36. *Ordinary General Meetings* – The society shall in each year hold two ordinary general meetings, one of which meetings shall be called the AGM.

52. *Committee of Management* – The business of the society shall be conducted by a Committee of Management, which, until the first ordinary general meeting is held, shall consist of the founding members, and after such meeting shall consist of no less than 9 but no more than 15 committeemen appointed at such meeting. The number of the committeemen may be altered from time to time by any general meeting on a motion of which at least 14 clear days' notice has been given to every member. Of the committeemen, three shall be elected solely by the employees of and contributors to the newspaper published by the society, the remainder being elected by the society in general meeting. The committee may from time to time co-opt for any period any suitable persons, whether members of the society or not, to serve on the committee and may remove such persons and such persons may take part in the deliberations of the committee and vote at any meetings thereof. No more than three such persons shall serve on the committee at any one time. For purposes of these rules and of the Act (the Industrial and Provident Societies Act, governing co-ops) such persons shall not be included in the expression 'committeemen' or 'members of the committee'.

(The word 'men' is used for legal purposes only, and means 'people'.)

93. *Application of Profits* – The profits of the society shall be applied as follows:-

a) Firstly, in paying interest on the share capital at such rate (not exceeding £5 per cent per annum) as may be recommended by the Committee and approved by the AGM.

94. *Employees' Share of Profits:-*

i) The proportion of profits due to an employee shall be credited to the recipient as share capital, until he holds five fully paid up shares, whereupon he may withdraw half of any further allocation, while the remaining half will be credited to him as share capital, until such time as the shareholding is £100 more than the minimum share holding, when any future allocation under this rule may be withdrawn in full.

It is worth adding that in a letter to the author in November 1981 the Co-operative Union (the federal body mainly representing the consumer co-op movement) expressed a willingness 'to be of assistance in producing rules for (a co-operative community radio station) and also arranging for their registration'. The Co-operative Union may be contacted via the Deputy General Secretary, Holyoake House, Hanover Street, Manchester M60 0AS – Tel: 061-852 4300.

Further advice and information on co-operative constitutions may be obtained from the National Co-operative Development Agency, 20 Albert Embankment, London SE1 7TJ – Tel: 01-211 4202. Or local Co-operative Development Agencies which can be contacted via Local Co-op Development Agencies Network, 43 Nansen Road, London SW11 – Tel: 01-748 3020 x 5331 (daytime) or 01-223 6220.

The *East End News* may be contacted via 17 Victoria Park Square, London E2 9PE – Tel: 01-981 7337.

Technical specifications for a community station

Studio Installations

Design philosophy

As already mentioned, the essence of a community radio station is that its resources should be available for all members of the community to use. Many potential users will have no previous experience of using radio broadcasting equipment, so it is important not to arouse needless fears about this. It is therefore essential to our suggested design philosophy that the external appearance of the equipment should be no more complicated or imposing than is absolutely necessary. The flashy technological image of the professional radio or recording studio is quite the opposite impression the community station should convey.

The aim of the design and choice of equipment should be that any reasonably intelligent person should feel able and confident to use the technical equipment after only a short period of training and practice. What follows should be seen as general guidelines for discussion and further investigation, rather than definitive proposals.

Choice of equipment

Choosing equipment does pose problems. Some professional broadcasting equipment, besides being highly expensive, is too sophisticated for the needs described here, and is intended for use by a professionally trained operator. Domestic equipment, on the other hand, is much cheaper and more familiar, but isn't nearly robust enough and lacks many useful facilities.

Suitable equipment does exist, but modifications and adaptations may have to be carried out to suit the peculiar needs of the station. Some items, like the sound mixing desks, are probably best custom-built, so that only appropriate facilities need to be provided, and any redundant complication can be left out.

Space and resources

It is presupposed that much of the output of the station will be originated in the studio itself: discussion, talk, interviews, drama and

poetry, children's programmes, live music. All these types of programmes can take a lot of time to prepare: many hours of studio
time could be used to produce an item which only runs for a few
minutes on the air. Although not all productions need such elaborate preparation – indeed, the enterprise can uniquely benefit from
live spontaneity – it should be borne in mind that a lot of studio time
is always needed over and above that used in live broadcasting.
Space and resources are continually needed to prepare, record or
edit material. Ideally this space should be available at all hours of
the day and night, including while the station is on the air. It should
be possible for the premises to be readily accessible during 'anti-
social' hours.

Suggested Layout

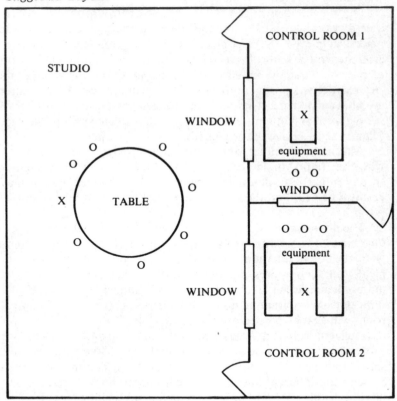

X – programme presenter   O – interviewee or guests

The figure shows a possible scheme for laying out the studio side
of the station, taking into account the sort of premises likely to be

available for the job. We have concerned ourselves only with the broadcasting areas themselves – obviously there will be a need for informal gathering space, office and storage room – but exactly how they will fit round the studio complex will be determined principally by the nature of the building where the studio is to be accommodated.

The term 'studio' is loosely used to describe two different types of space. There is the technical area – which we shall call the 'control room' – where all the taperecording machines, record decks and technical controls are housed. Then there is the studio area proper – a large space, relatively devoid of technical apparatus – where microphones can be set up for discussions, drama, music and so on. This area, which is supervised technically from the control room, will simply be referred to as the 'studio'.

Our suggested arrangement shows two control rooms, each capable of working on its own and independently of the other. If the person in charge of the controls is also the presenter of the programme, this is known as a 'self-operated' programme. This form of operation is most suited to 'DJ' (disc-jockey) programmes and straightforward productions where the demands on the presenter are not too involved. Under these arrangements, a small number of people, probably no more than three, can also take part in the programme as interviewees or contributors.

Alternatively, either of the two control rooms can also work with the studio for larger-scale productions, where the presenter speaks from the studio, and an operator, whose voice may or may not also be heard on the air, operates the equipment in the control room.

The doubling-up of control rooms has a number of advantages. One control room can be used to set-up or record a programme while the other is on the air. If one control room suffers from a technical fault or requires maintenance, the other can take over its duties. Training can take place more easily and will not have to wait until outside programme hours. People trained to use one control room will also be able to use the other.

Each control room is equipped with a mixing desk, three record decks, two taperecorders, and two cartridge players for jingles, short trails etc. The control rooms will also accommodate up to three or four microphones as required. The studio will have a circular table with a microphone in the middle, plus facilities for plugging in a fairly large number of microphones and headphones if necessary.

All the areas where microphones will be used must have appropriate sound proofing and sound treatment. The sound proofing is to prevent sounds from outside entering the studio, and to prevent sounds from leaking from one studio or control room to another. The sound treatment involves modifying the acoustics of the rooms, so that they do not sound unduly hollow, resonant or boomy. Sometimes heavy carpets, curtains, and soft furnishings are sufficient, but ideally more elaborate measures, using specially designed absorbers, should be taken.

Recording studio

The provisions just described would be quite sufficient for the day-to-day operations of the station. Further facilities might be thought desirable for more ambitious projects. Another control room and studio could be contemplated, being primarily designed for recording, rather than live transmission. This would have more sophisticated microphone and taperecording facilities, and could provide a less hectic environment in which people could work more carefully.

Editing

Most recorded material, especially interviews and news recordings, benefits from being edited before it is broadcast. An editing cubicle – a small room or area with two taperecorders – where people could go to listen to, splice or dub recordings, would be a very useful resource. If the station has a news room area, this also ought to be equipped with a taperecorder for listening to tapes.

Logging tapes

The keeping of logging tapes – a recording of all the broadcasts made by the station – might be a legal requirement, or it might be thought advisable anyway. This requires a taperecorder to be modified to run at a very slow speed, recording the station's output and a timing signal, such as the Speaking Clock, simultaneously. These tapes would be kept for a period of time, say three months, and could be referred to if the need arose.

Stereo

If the VHF band is used for broadcasting, it would easily be possible to broadcast in stereo. However, producing original material in stereo can be very complicated, requiring considerable technical skill and expertise. But taperecorders and record decks are generally built for stereo rather than mono, and the extra equipment needed to broadcast a stereo signal is comparatively simple and inexpensive. It is recommended, therefore, that 'token stereo' be adopted in the main control rooms. This means that if any material, such as gramophone records, is originally recorded in stereo, it will pass

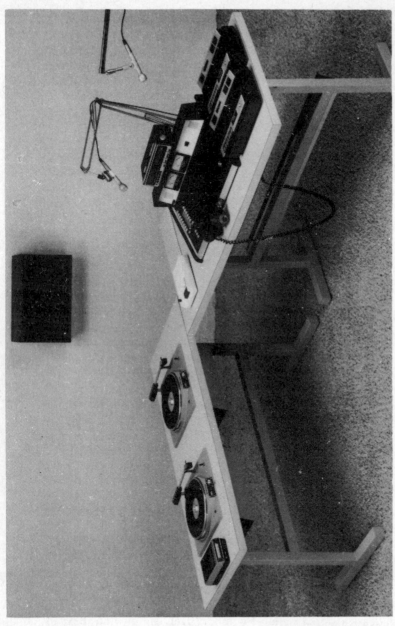

Canadian Broadcasting Corporation remote-community radio package layout – the equipment is arranged for announcer operation by unskilled person.

through the system in stereo and be broadcast as such. However, there will be no facilities for generating original stereo material in the on-air control rooms, except possibly in the 'recording' studio/ control room, if available.

The great advantage of a 'token stereo' outfit is that it is no more complicated, from the operator's point of view, than mono equipment – virtually no extra controls are required.

Medium frequency broadcasting

Broadcasting on the medium waveband, although restricted to mono, has a few compensations, described more fully in the section on transmission. The less exacting reproduction available from a medium frequency (MF) system means that the performance of the studio equipment, and the precision with which it is manipulated, can be considerably relaxed. Domestic cassette taperecorders, for instance, can be used liberally on medium wave transmissions, even in studio production, without adverse comment from listeners. Fairly poor technical quality, such as would be immediately apparent to any moderately critical VHF listener, will pass unnoticed on MF. So minor savings on studio equipment would be possible if MF transmission were used, although they would probably be no larger than to offset the additional costs of the MF transmitter.

Outside sources

Both BBC and IBA local radio stations have a variety of outside sources more or less permanently wired into their studio equipment. These may be radio car signals from special receivers, or landline signals from remote microphones located in the offices of local services such as the police, the road and public transport organisations, or in sports grounds, council chambers etc. Although it is unlikely that a community station will be able to afford a radio car, it is possible that the station may wish to send staff to a limited number of remote points in its area, where live broadcasting may take place from time to time.

For this to happen, it is necessary for the remote location to be linked to the studio by two landlines, which may be rented temporarily or, more likely, permanently from the Post Office. The line sending signals from the remote location back to the studios should be of high quality: it is known as a 'music' line. The other line travelling in the other direction need only be of telephone-like quality, known as a 'speech' circuit. This line provides 'cue and talkback' – that is, a feed of the programme coming from the studio, interrupted as necessary by instructions from the person back at the station.

Charges for these circuits vary according to their length, but over distances involved in community radio they are unlikely to exceed £150 per year, and could well be much less.

The studio equipment must, of course, be capable of controlling the output from all outside sources, including an ordinary telephone line or lines (for 'phone-in' programmes). The equipment must also be able to send the appropriate signals to the person at the far end.

Transmission check

It is imperative that the studio is equipped with some means of checking that the signal being broadcast from the transmitter is of satisfactory quality. A high quality receiver, tuned to the station's own broadcasts, is an indispensable part of the station's equipment. The output from this receiver must be available on the operator's headphone and loudspeaker circuits at all times. It would also be desirable for this receiver's output to be heard throughout the station building, not only for the convenience of staff, guests and visitors, but also so that any fault is immediately noticed.

The studio equipment must give a clear visual indication to the operator of any malfunction at the transmitter. The control desks should also be able to instruct the transmitter to turn on and off, or to switch from stereo to mono operation, giving visual confirmation that this has taken place.

Some idea of equipment costs

Control Rooms (on air)

6 studio record decks....................................	£2,520		
4 tape machines (record/replay).......................	3,600		
2 mixing desks with ancillary controls................	3,000		
4 cartridge machines....................................	3,000		
5 microphones...	600		
2 pairs of monitor speakers............................	600		
Headphones, clocks, microphones, stands, telephone balance unit, compressor/limiter, monitor receiver etc.....................................	1,800	*Total:*	£15,120

Studio (on air)

1 pair monitor loudspeakers...........................	300		
2 omni-directional microphones.......................	300		
5 cardioid microphones.................................	600		
Headphones, clock, microphone stands etc........	600	*Total*	£1,800

Control Room (recording)

1 studio record player.....................................	420
3 tape machines (record/replay).......................	2,700

1 editing tape machine....................................	360		
1 mixing desk with equaliser etc.......................	2,400		
1 pair monitor loudspeakers............................	300		
Headphones, clock, stopwatch, compressor/			
limiter, effects unit etc...................................	1,800	*Total:*	£7,980

Studio (recording)

1 pair monitor speakers.................................	300		
2 omni-directional microphones......................	300		
10 cardioid microphones...............................	1,200	*Total:*	£1,800

Grand Total: £26,700, to which must be added the cost of the building conversions and the actual installation of equipment itself, which could easily amount to a further £12,000-24,000, depending on how much voluntary work went on, what sort of premises were envisaged etc.

It should be emphasised, however, that this list is only intended as a very general guide.

Transmission

VHF or medium wave transmitter?

No indication has yet been forthcoming from the Home Office about which broadcast band will be available for community radio, if and when such operations are licensed. There are two broadcast bands in the UK which are techncially suitable for various types of small-scale radio: they are the VHF-FM band, and the MF band, more popularly known as medium wave.

Let us briefly examine the technical characteristics of each band. Medium wave is by far the oldest of the two systems, but still accounts for over three-quarters of all UK radio listening. There are various reasons put forward for this: firstly, a wider choice of programmes is available on medium wave; secondly, all transistor radios can pick up this band, while only some have VHF; thirdly, reception on medium wave, although of inferior quality, is less critical of location and receiver performance than reception on VHF.

Medium frequency broadcasting does have one very important disadvantage – reception at night is marred by foreign broadcasts from Europe and North Africa, owing to a phenomenon known as 'sky-wave' reception. This means that from about an hour before sunset until about an hour after sunrise the following morning, foreign broadcasting stations can be heard on every frequency in the band, and only those local stations which are very strong have much chance of blotting them out. So a signal from a community station may be heard very clearly during the day, but at night, reception in areas not very close to the transmitter will be liable to be submerged by foreign interference.

The 'day' and 'night' periods obviously vary according to the season; in the depth of winter, a frequency may only be clear of interference from 9am until 3pm, at the equinoxes (with British Summer Time in force) the channel may be usable from 8am until 6pm, while near the Summer solstice the frequency may be clear from before 6am until after 8pm.

Set beside this major disadvantage are two principal advantages: firstly, everyone in the target area is likely to have a receiver capable of picking up the broadcasts; secondly, the lower quality of the transmission medium means that any shortcomings in the studio equipment, or the recordings played, are likely to pass unnoticed by the audience. So too are many operational errors, such as maladjustment of signal levels, because an automatic level control circuit can be usefully employed on medium wave, although such a circuit would produce unacceptable results on VHF.

So in essence medium wave broadcasting is a more rough-and-ready process than VHF transmission, and although the programmes can only be received in mono, and not very hi-fi mono at that, there is no evidence to suggest that this factor is leading to mass public desertions from the medium.

VHF transmission, on the other hand, is capable of very high quality transmission indeed, and it is straightforward and not very costly to broadcast all or part of the programme content in stereo. VHF waves travel in a more or less line-of-sight path from the transmitter, and are easily blocked by hills, tall buildings, or other physical obstructions. This factor can sometimes be exploited to ensure that the service reaches only those areas which it is intended to serve, by judicious choice of the transmitting site and aerial characteristics.

While the coverage of a VHF service is generally easier to confine to a specific area, the quality of reception on the outer edges of the reception area is likely to be patchy. Listeners living high up a building (even only one or two floors above ground), on the side facing the transmitter, will be able to hear the service quite clearly, while the others on the ground floor or basement, facing the other direction, may find that little or nothing can be picked up. This problem can be completely alleviated by the erection of a suitable rooftop aerial, but the cost (about £30), and the fact that this will confine the receiver to operation in only one or two fixed locations, may deter all but the most enthusiastic listeners.

However, without carrying out field tests it is impossible to determine exactly how much power or for medium wave what aerial characteristics will provide the desired coverage.

Transmitter reliability and maintenance

Low power transmitters and their aerials do not have highly stressed components, and it is likely that they will be able to operate without attention for long periods of time. The equipment used will be no larger than an average suitcase, and apart from requiring a mains supply and a weatherproof location secure from vandalism, there are no special environmental problems. The maintenance of the transmitter and associated equipment will be the responsibility of the supplier, and it is likely that a maintenance contract could be agreed to this effect.

Costs

The cost of the transmitter and aerial is small compared to the cost of conversion, installation, and equipment involved in the studio. At present prices, we think it unlikely to exceed £6,000 (for VHF) or £7,800 (for MF). To this, however, must be added the costs of carrying out engineering tests and surveys – possibly £600 – and any site costs which may be incurred.

Further sources of information

A detailed study of *The Technical Feasibility of Community Radio in London* was commissioned by COMCOM in November 1979 from Fred Wise, former IBA Head of Network and Service Planning Department. The report found room in the VHF band for 12 or so 3-4Km radius stations, or about half that number of stations covering a sector of the city, or one London-wide communtiy of interest station. It also provides detailed information on field strengths and channel separation etc. Available from COMCOM Publications, see section 5 for details.

Norman McLeod, technical consultant to the National Association of Student Broadcasting, who wrote this section along with Tim Foulsham, an ex-BBC radio engineer. They specialise in the design and production of low-cost, low-technology radio studios and transmitters, and are available for consultation via:

Wireless Workshop, Unit 10, Beaconsfield Workshops, 63 Beaconsfield Road, Brighton BN1 4QJ. Tel: 0273 671928

Where to contact radio workshops and community radio projects

BASEMENT PROJECT
St. Georges Town Hall, Cable Street, London E1   Tel: 01-790 4020
Contact: Tony Crisp
Concentrates on making programmes with young people.

INTER-ACTION AUDIO-VISUAL UNIT
15 Wilkin Street, London NW5 3NG   Tel:01-267 9421
Contact: Pete Mount
Working with young people with a Radio Van linked to access spot on BBC Radio London. Hope to launch a National Young People's Radio Club Network in 1982.

ISLINGTON RADIO PROJECT
Islington Bus Co., Palmer Place, London N7   Tel: 01-609 0226/7
Contact: Carlos Ordonez
See chapter 4.

LOCAL RADIO WORKSHOP
12 Praed Mews, London W2   Tel:01-402 7651
Contact: Gloria George
Help groups make tapes with object of getting them broadcast on local stations throughout the UK.
Have just published monitoring survey of local radio in London.

RADIO BETHNAL GREEN
Oxford House, Derbyshire Street, Bethnal Green, London E2 Tel: 01-739 9855
Contact: Dave Clark
Workshop for the Bethnal Green area.

WOOLWICH SIMBA PROJECT
48 Artillery Place, Woolwich, London SE18   Tel: 01-317 0451
Contact: Nick Darnell
Emphasis on youth and music.

BRISTOL URBAN RADIO PROJECT
Bristol CSV Centre, 13 Midland Road, St Philips, Bristol BS2 0JT
Tel: 0272 552968
Contact: Janet Atfield
Community liaison/back-up service for BBC Radio Bristol, and community training production centre.

COMMONSOUND
Commonground Resources Centre, 87 The Wicker, Sheffield S3 8HT
Tel:0742 738572
Contact: Chris Meade
See chapter 4.

COMMUNITY EDUCATION CENTRE
4 Queensferry Street, Edinburgh   Tel: 031-225 9451
Contact: Alan Mercer
Community training facility.

COMMUNITY PROGRAMMES WORKSHOP
Hull College of Higher Education, Cottingham Road, Hull, North Humberside HU6 7RT   Tel: 0482 42157
Contact: Peter Adamson
Studios and training in radio production for groups. Suitable programmes broadcast through BBC Radio Humberside.

MILTON KEYNES RADIO WORKSHOP
The Old Rectory, Peartree Lane, Woughton on the Green, Milton Keynes
Tel: 0908 678514
Contact: Roger Kitchen
Concentrate on running training workshops for young people and community groups, which were closely connected to the cable station until its recent closure.

MERSEYSIDE VISUAL COMMUNICATIONS UNIT
90-92 Whitechapel, Liverpool L1 6EN   Tel: 051-709 9460
Contact: Colin Wilkinson
Sound studio and record label, mainly used to make low cost demo records for local bands. Hope to start young people's media unit in early 1982.

RADIO DOOM
PO Box 18, Southport, Merseyside PR8 1JP   Tel: 051-228 8894
Part of a community multi-media project.

SUNDERLAND RADIO WORKSHOP
c/o Community Arts Project Sunderland, St Ignatius Precinct, Hendon, Sunderland   Tel: 0783 41214
Contact: Mick Catmull
Trains community groups to make programmes.

SWINDON VIEWPOINT
*c/o Thamesdown Film Workshop, The Arts Centre, Devizes Road,
Swindon, Wilts.*
Contact: Martin Parry

Making community radio and TV programmes for the local cable system
and perhaps for the forthcoming commercial radio station.

WEST YORKSHIRE RADIO ACTION
1st Floor Office, Wellington House, 67 Wellington Street, Leeds LS1 4LZ
Tel: 0532 443647
Contact: Lynda Syed & John Callaghan

A Community Service Volunteer project developing the use of local radio to
stimulate voluntary action and self-help activity, working in partnership
with local radio stations and councils for voluntary service.

YORKSHIRE ARTS ASSOCIATION
Communications Centre, 21 Chapel Street, Bradford 1   Tel: 0274 22769
Contact: D. Bower

Equipment and studios for hire to individuals and non-commercial groups.

Community Radio Station Projects

HOUNSLOW COMMUNITY RADIO
1 Treaty Road, Hounslow TW3 1DX   Tel: 01-570 1168/9
Contact: I.S. Uppal
See chapter 4.

LONDON OPEN RADIO
2 Warwick Crescent, London W2   Tel:01-289 7163
Contact: Peter Bevington

Group seeking licence for London-wide community of interest station, particularly youth, progressive music and minorities. Seeks members and volunteers, has organiser funded through the MSC's Community Enterprise
Programme. Also good point of contact for progressive London radio
pirates, and have published interesting submission to the Home Office.

EAST LONDON RADIO CAMPAIGN
129 Henniker Gardens, East Ham, London E6
Contact: Phil Troll

WASHINGTON RADIO GROUP
*c/o Washington Development Corporation, Usworth Hall, Stephenson,
District 12, Washington, Tyne and Wear NE37 3HS*
Tel:0632 463591 x 224
Contact: Marilyn Charlton

Group exploring possibility of setting up Washington radio or getting access
slots on existing local radio.

BRAY COMMUNITY RADIO
c/o 82 Charnwood, Bray, Co. Wicklow, Eire
Tel: 0001 (from London) – 868583 (9am-5pm) 0001-868690 (after 6pm)
Contact: John Murphy

Interesting semi-legal (due to peculiarities in Eire's broadcasting laws) community station, which also provides excellent point for contacting the Irish community radio movement.

For up-to-date information about workshops and radio station projects contact Joan Munro organiser of the Gulbenkian Foundation's Community Communications Development Project – who would also be pleased to provide advice and help on setting up such facilities. See section 6 for address.

Cable Radio Stations

GREENWICH SOUND
154 Plumstead Road, London SE18   Tel: 01-317 8584
Contact: Terry Barnes

RADIO BASILDON
South Gunnels, Basildon, Essex SS14 1H   Tel: 0268 416256
Contact: Margaret Ballard

RADIO THAMESMEAD
19 Tavy Bridge, Abbey Wood, London SE2 9UG   Tel: 01-310 5025/9400
Contact: Frank Warren

All the cable stations above welcome volunteer helpers. Good place to gain practical experience if you're near one.

WALWORTH CABLE RADIO
c/o Walworth & Aylesbury Community Arts Trust, Shop 8, Taplow,
Aylesbury Estate, London SE17   Tel: 01-701 9010
Contact: Caroline Mitchell

Group at present running radio workshop, hope eventually to run their own cable station.

HASTINGS COMMUNITY RADIO
c/o Hastings Community Service Council, Bolton Tomson House, 49
Cambridge Gardens, Hastings TN34 1EN   Tel: 0424 426162
Contact: Roger Puffett

Proposed community cable station to be operated by a Youth Opportunities Programme under the auspices of the Hastings Community Service Council.

Useful publications

RELAY
See note 6, chapter 4 for details.
Box 12, 2A St. Paul's Road, London N1. Single copies 60p, Annual sub. 4 issues £2 individuals, £5 institutions.

ANOTHER STANDARD
Bi-monthly national newsletter of the community arts movement. Issue Jan/Feb 1982 carried a useful supplement on community radio.
48 Grange Terrace, Pelton Fell, Chester le Street, Co. Durham DH2 2DP. Annual sub. 6 issues £3.

HOW TO USE YOUR LOCAL RADIO STATION
Information bulletin prepared by BBC TV's Grapevine programme with help from Simon Partridge and COMCOM. Gives advice on how to get access, plus useful contacts and lists all stations on air.
Grapevine, BBC TV, London W12 8QT. Free with large SAE.

THE LOCAL RADIO KIT
A new practical guide which explains: what local radio can do; how to get your local station interested in your programme; who to contact and how to contact them. And helps you to: get a clear message across; gain confidence; make your own programme. Kit contains: a handbook, instructional card game and demonstration cassette. Published jointly by Community Service Volunteers and the National Extension College at £5.95.

THE DIRECTORY OF MEDIA TRAINING OPPORTUNITIES
The most comprehensive guide to part-time media training courses available in the UK. Courses listed include: how to make your own radio or TV programme; where to learn audio-visual techniques; interviewing and being interviewed; scriptwriting; community arts and printing. Presented by geographical area with full details of facilities and fees. Published by Community Service Volunteers at £2.

Both the above publications from CSV, 237 Pentonville Road, London N1. Special offer – both publications at £6.95. All prices include p&p.

HOW TO USE A TAPE RECORDER FOR COMMUNITY PROJECTS
A practical guide on how to use a tape recorder with community groups which would be useful for training in radio workshops or for those seeking access to local radio.
Forthcoming from Inter-Action Inprint, 15 Wilkin Street, London NW5 3NG.

USING THE MEDIA
Handbook on how to deal with the press, TV and radio. Description of how the system works with detailed tips on contacting journalists, press releases,

radio interviews, news conferences, TV appearances, phone-ins, access programmes and directory of newspapers and broadcasting organisations. Published by Pluto Press, available from bookshops at £2.50 and excellent
value.

THE TECHNICAL FEASIBILITY OF COMMUNITY RADIO IN LONDON
See end of section 3 for details.
COMCOM Publications, 92 Huddleston Road, London N7 0EG. £1 incl.
p&p. Cheques/POs payable to 'Community Communications Group'.

THE COMMUNITY RADIO SUPPORTERS' OPEN LETTER TO THE HOME SECRETARY
Comments on the 3rd report of the Home Office Local Radio Working Party.
From COMCOM Publications above. 75p incl. p&p.

A COMMUNITY RADIO STATION FOR THE HOUNSLOW AREA
A feasibility study and guidelines for setting up a community station, covering: introduction explaining the need; background context; general principles of a community station; organisational structure and functions; establishing the station; location and operation; finance; studio installations;
transmitters; footnotes; appendices; up-to-date postscript.
Compiled and published by Simon Partridge and available from him at the
COMCOM address (cheques/POs payable to him) at £5 incl. p&p.

ANARCHIST REVIEW
Issue 5 contained detailed instructions on building a cheap radio trans-
mitter.
Cienfuegos Press, Over the Water, Sanday, Orkney. £2 plus p&p.

UNDERCURRENTS/RADICAL TECHNOLOGY
Issues 7 and 8 had articles on d-i-y radio as does their book Radical Techno-
logy.
Details from 27 Clerkenwell Close, London EC1.

ALTERNATIVE LONDON No.6
New completely revised edition published early 1982, contains informative
section on alternative arts and media – including community radio, ham
radio, pirates and CB.
From bookshops or Alternative London, BCM Alter, London WC1N 3XX.
Excellent value at £3.50.

THE RADIO DIRECTORY
A comprehensive bi-annual guide to the UK radio industry. Includes sections on student, hospital and cable stations, plus some information on
community and alternative organisations. Listings are free.
Published jointly by Radio Month and Hamilton House Publishing. Editorial: HHP, Grooms Lane, Creaton, Northampton NN6 8NN. Subs. Radio
Month, 107 Dawes Road, London SW6. Single copy £4.50, annual sub. £9.

BRITISH FILM INSTITUTE PUBLICATIONS
127 Charing Cross Road, London WC2H 0EA.

DEVELOPMENT DIALOGUE: 1981 NO.2 – 'Towards a New World Information and Communication Order'
Just published, this is the most comprehensive and theoretically sophisticated

case for alternative communications we know of. Among other things it contains a fascinating introduction on 'The Right to Inform and be Informed', and substantial papers on 'The Democratization of Communications', 'Advertising and the Democratization of Communications', and 'A Model for Democratic Communication'. Although focussed on the Third Systems (i.e. those not directly controlled by the state or unbridled profit-orientated market forces) of the Third World, much of what it has to say is of direct relevance to those involved in community radio and media. Available free on request from: Dag Hammarskjöld Foundation, Övre Slottsgatan 2, S-752 20 Uppsala, Sweden.

Useful organisations

COMMUNITY RADIO GROUP, COMCOM
92 Huddleston Road, London N7 0EG   Tel: 01-263 6692 (answerphone)
Contact: Simon Partridge

Founded in 1977, a national network of individuals and groups lobbying for community stations run as listener/producer co-ops or non-profit public trusts. If you want to join or get publications list send SAE.

COMMUNITY COMMUNICATIONS DEVELOPMENT PROJECT
Gulbenkian Foundation, 5 Tavistock Place, London WC1H 9SS
Tel: 01-387 7719/7341
Contact: Joan Munro

Provides information and advice about a variety of community media, with a particular emphasis on radio. Pump-priming grants are also available, write for details.

BROADCASTING AS PUBLIC SERVICE
Address and phone as Joan Munro above.
Contact: Philip Adams

Provides information and practical assistance to community and voluntary groups so that they can influence the shape of new commercial local radio stations. Also encourages greater access and accountability in broadcasting services generally.

CAMPAIGN FOR PRESS AND BROADCASTING FREEDOM
274/288 London Road, Hadleigh, Essex SS7 2DE   Tel: 0702 553131
Contact: John Jennings

So far has concentrated mainly on securing a 'right of reply' in the press, but has recently broadened its aims to take in broadcasting. Campaign has wide labour movement backing.

NATIONAL ASSOCIATION OF HOSPITAL BROADCASTING ORGANISATIONS
56 Fleet Road, Benfleet, Essex   Tel: 03745 3256
Contact: Alf Partridge

The federal body representing the hospital radio stations throughout the UK. Provides information and advice on hospital broadcasting.

NATIONAL ASSOCIATION OF STUDENT BROADCASTING
University Radio Warwick, University of Warwick, Coventry, Warks.
CV4 7AL   Tel: 0203 24011 x 2020
Contact: Hazel Westwood

The federal body representing student broadcasting, will provide information and advice.

MEDIA DEVELOPMENT OFFICE
Community Service Volunteers, 237 Pentonville Road, London N1 9NJ
Tel: 01-278 6601
Contact: Jo Simpson

Provides help so voluntary and community groups can use the media more effectively, particularly local radio. Has some regional/local offices.

THE MEDIA PROJECT
The Volunteer Centre, 29 Lower Kings Road, Berkhamsted, Herts HP4 2AB   Tel: 04427 73311
Contact: Eileen Ware/Mike Hodgkinson

Information, advice and research service for people working in the area of social action broadcasting (i.e. using broadcasting to encourage activity rather than passivity). Produces informative quarterly bulletin and other publications on subscription annually of £4.

YOUNG ADULT MEDIA UNIT
National Extension College, 18 Brooklands Avenue, Cambridge CB2 2HN   Tel: 0223 63465
Contact: John Meed

Promotes links between broadcasters and young people, and helps local projects get going.

CARDIFF RADIO TRUST
Radio House, West Canal Wharf, Cardiff CF1 5XJ   Tel: 0222 45599
Contact: Simon White

Democratically elected group who own 50% of CBC, Cardiff's commercial station. They elect half of CBC's Board of Directors and are responsible for community input.

COVENTRY RADIO ACTION GROUP
138 Hornall Lane East, Coventry
Contact: Roger Zarm

Pressure group campaigning for more accessible and accountable local radio in the Midlands.

GWENT BROADCASTING TRUST
Polypill, 35 Commercial Road, Newport, Gwent NPT 2PB
Tel: 0633 56307/53705
Contact: Martin Cummella

Made unsuccessful community bid for Newport commercial station, now establishing own radio workshop. See chapter 4.

RADIO ACTION
23A High Street, Inverness   Tel: 0463 37696 or 22 44 33
Contact: Peter Peacock or Ishbell McLellan

Holds shares and seats on the board of Moray Firth Radio and encourages community involvement in the station.

ABERDEEN BROADCASTING ASSOCIATION
264 Queens Road, Aberdeen   Tel: 0224 35039 (home) 0224 26688 (office)
Contact: Elizabeth Garrett

Made unsuccessful community bid for Aberdeen commercial radio franchise in 1979, but still interested in encouraging greater community involvement in both BBC and IBA local broadcasting.

YORKSHIRE MEDIA GROUP
229 Woodhouse Lane, Leeds LS2 9LF   Tel: 0532 448921
Contact: Geoff Hill

Grew out of failed community bid for Leeds commercial station. Has close links with community groups and labour movement, aims to increase media accountability and raise public awareness of media uses in Yorkshire.

BLACK CONNECTION
c/o 64 Mount Pleasant, Liverpool L3 5SH
Contact: Alex Bennet

Group doing weekly programme for black people on Liverpool's commercial station. Have produced interesting report on their experience from which others interested in doing the same could learn a lot.

BLACK WOMEN'S RADIO GROUP
c/o 75 Synder Road, Stoke Newington, London N16
Contact: Ingrid Lewis

Want to pass on technical skills to other black women and men, and record the activities and experiences of black people.

WOMEN'S AIR WAVES
c/o Local Radio Workshop, 12 Praed Mews, London W2 1QY
Tel: 01-402 7651

A closed group who make feminist programmes with and about women, mostly magazine/current affairs. Will advise other women who want to start their own radio group.

STRANGELOVE
c/o Local Radio Workshop, as above.
Contact: Ruth Sabey

Group making radio programmes which are anti-nuclear.

MEDIAWATCH
c/o 104 Constantine Road, London NW3   Tel: 01-267 5806
Contact: Ruth Sabey

Group monitoring media on nuclear issues and helping anti-nuclear groups to use the media.

ALTERNATIVE BREAKERS COLLECTIVE
Box ABC, ITM, 44 Albion Road, Sutton, Surrey
(or one four for Mister Natural in the Islington twenty, London)

A loose network of politically and religiously non-aligned people who want to keep CB free from bureaucratic and police control. Operates alternative info exchange network.

COMMUNICATIONS FOR DEVELOPMENT FOUNDATION (CODEV)
c/o IFDA, 2 Place du Marche, CH-1260 Nyon, Switzerland
Tel: (41-22)-618282
Contact: Michael Z. Cutajar

The newly established international clearing house and development agency for those engaged in developing participatory, non-commercial media, particularly in the Third World. One of their first tasks will be to draw up an 'inventory of alternative communications' with which CODEV could work, and to help these projects communicate with each other. In this spirit why not get in touch, and let others learn from your experience.

Glossary

BBC – The British Broadcasting Corporation was established in 1927 out of the British Broadcasting Company, which was owned by a consortium of wireless manufacturers and had been granted a monopoly on providing programmes by the Post Office in 1922 provided it did not carry advertising (although it was occasionally allowed to broadcast sponsored programmes).

IBA – The Independent Broadcasting Authority was established in 1954 as the Independent Television Authority to regulate commercial TV when it was introduced. It became the IBA when it added commercial radio to its responsibilities in 1972.

CB – Citizens' Band radio – This is a two-way radio communication service available to technically unqualified members of the public with the minimum of fuss and formality. A licence for UK CB operation costs £10 and is available from any Post Office.

CB was originally conceived in the United States, and was subsequently authorised in a number of other countries. It was only recently legalised in the UK after a concerted campaign and much illegal operation.

Two-way transceivers (rigs) are available for £50 upwards. Most equipment works on 27MHz, though the 934MHz band is also available at much higher cost for more private and better quality contact. Rigs are available for home-based, mobile or hand portable use. Beware of cheap (under £50 each) hand-held sets – these are usually only 'toys' with a very limited range and terrible audio quality.

You can expect a range of a mile or so from a good hand-held pair of transceivers, up to five miles from vehicle to vehicle, and ten miles or more from home based stations. The range is restricted by tall buildings and built-up areas, and increases in open country. In many parts of the UK the 27Mhz frequencies are heavily occupied by both legal operators and 'pirates' – running high power equipment in an attempt to contact long-distance stations. On the legal bands there are few restrictions on the use to which CB may be put, and even these are widely disregarded.

CB users broadly divide into two camps – those who use it in a strictly utilitarian way for traffic information, directions, business conversations etc. and those who are enthusiasts and take a great interest in the medium in its own right. A number of specialist publications – *What CB, Breaker, CB Radio, CB World* etc. cater for various associated lifestyles and interests.

VHF – Very High Frequency – This refers to radio frequencies between 30 and 300 MHz, though in broadcasting terms it means the band between 88 and 108 MHz, which is assigned internationally to broadcasting stations, and is available on many (but not all) of the radio sets in use.

VHF broadcasting permits very high quality reception, in stereo if required, but it is more critical of receiver quality and location than the older medium and long wave system. Most broadcasts on VHF in the UK are duplicated on medium and long wave, although Open University and other educational programmes, plus some Radio 3 programmes during Test Matches, are only broadcast on VHF.

Powerful VHF transmitters have a range of no more than 50-100 miles, and it is fairly easy to use low power equipment to confine a service to a small area of a few miles' diameter. At this power level aerials for transmitting are small and unobtrusive, and transmitting equipment is also small and relatively inexpensive.

In the UK only the segments 88-97.6 and 102.1-104 MHz are currently released by the Home Office for broadcasting, despite international agreement that broadcasting is the primary service over the whole band from 88-108 MHz.

Committees on the Future of Broadcasting – about every 10 years an ad hoc committee to look into the future of broadcasting is established. Indeed the BBC was set up as the result of the Crawford Committee of 1925. This was followed by Ullswater in 1935, Beveridge in 1949, Pilkington in 1960 and Annan in 1977 (he would have reported earlier but his first attempt in 1972 was cancelled by an incoming Tory government).

Opt-out – An opt-out station is a small local relay station which is allowed to broadcast its own programmes for a limited time each day. At other times it will be rebroadcasting regional or national network radio. The BBC already has several such stations in Scotland and one in North East Wales and Northern Ireland.

Induction Loops – Induction loops are special aerials which radiate a magnetic field over a short distance. They are used for paging systems within a building, usually on long wave (low frequencies). It is also possible to obtain a licence for an inductive loop system operating on a frequency in the medium wave (MF) band. This can be used to broadcast parochial services to ordinary transistor radios within the confines of a particular institution, such as a hospital or university.

Although the broadcast quality from an inductive loop system is at least as good as a conventional MF radio station when it has been properly engineered, the system is expensive to install because the aerials have a short range and often a dozen or more may be needed to serve as few as a thousand students or patients. All the aerials have to be linked by cable to the transmitting system, which must comply with the relevant Home Office specification.

In addition, the licence fee for inductive systems is hefty, the initial charge being over £700, though dropping to £260 on annual renewal. This covers the cost of the technical tests involved in checking that the system is working to specification, including a requirement that the signal cannot be effectively received outside the confines of the institution for which the licence has been issued.

Video – is an electronic means of recording pictures and sounds on a magnetic tape, as in a taperecorder. Using a lightweight electronic camera together with a portable recorder you can record a video film. The resulting film can then be played back, instantly if required, on a TV set with a special adaptor. Such equipment first became widely and cheaply available in the early 1970s.

Community arts – is a very general term which refers to almost any non-commercial creative activity in which non-professionals take part alongside professionals (often generalist community arts workers) with the aim of enhancing self-expression and articulacy and helping towards individual and communal growth. Certain types of community radio could be seen as community arts and vice versa.

Access – is a vague term often used in a confusing way. For our purposes it means getting access to the broadcasting facilities of an existing local radio station, without having your message watered down by the media professionals employed there. This gives you the chance to air subjects the established media simply aren't interested in or positively avoid. Probably the best known example of this sort of programming is the 'Open Door' programmes on BBC-2 TV.

Opt-into – in contrast to an opt-out station an opt-into one retains its autonomy from the larger regional or national network, but comes to some mutually beneficial arrangement to use their programming at various times of the day.

Home Office Local Radio Working Party – was an ad hoc body consisting solely of Home Office, BBC and IBA officials established by the Labour Government after the publication of its White Paper on broadcasting in 1978. Its purpose was to carve up the airwaves between the BBC and IBA. COMCOM and others objected to its narrow terms of reference and to the fact that many important voices were being excluded from the debate about new developments in local broadcasting. The problems which both systems are now encountering seems to vindicate our stand. The Third Report may be obtained on request from the Home Office Broadcasting Department. See Chapter 5 note 8 for address.

Lakerism – 'laker' is a word that began to enter the English language in early 1982. It still has a somewhat ambiguous meaning ranging between the extremes of depicting the heroic, swash-buckling qualities of its owner as the fearless entrepreneur battling against the filthy state monopolies to serve 'everyperson'. On the other hand there are those who are equally convinced that it depicts the clever con-man who embarks on impossible business ventures and ends up losing everybody's money but his own. No doubt we must wait the judgement of history as to whether the word enters the dictionary as a term of abuse or praise. In the meantime for our purposes it means 'unfettered competition' a la Margaret Thatcher.

Frequencies for pilot community stations

(This is the text of Appendix 1 of the Community Radio Supporters' Open Letter to the Home Secretary.)

We propose first in this appendix to look at the future of the UK VHF broadcasting band during the years 1982 and 1983. We have deliberately narrowed the timescale under consideration for two reasons: a) because all those community interest stations seeking licences to operate a pilot service seem to be agreed that a one or two-year assignment will adequately suit their immediate purposes: to go on air for a sufficient length of time to define public demand for their respective services; and b) because the hitherto unpracticed art of examining frequency assignments in the short term, rather than as permanent entities, reveals possibilities which the conventional approach cannot uncover.

At the moment, the local radio sub-band from 94.8MHz contains 2.7MHz-worth of spectrum, and this band supports approximately 50 local radio services in England, including a number of high-power assignments in the major urban areas. It is less heavily used outside England, and we may take it that although the band is nearly 'full' in some parts of England, there are further longterm assignments available for BBC and IBA services in Scotland, Wales and Northern Ireland (HOLRWP report p23 para 5.16(b)).

The new broadcasting sub-band from 102.1-10.4MHz contains 1.9MHz-worth of spectrum, and it therefore follows that if this band is used exclusively for the development of local and/or community radio services, the amount of spectrum available for these purposes will increase by 70 per cent from 1 January 1982, subject to any restraints of an international nature which may apply in this part of the spectrum (p23 para 5.16 (b)).

The HOLRWP report suggests that there 'may well be' some new local radio services using assignments in the band 102.1-104MHz (p24 para 5.17). Conversely, one may conclude that there 'may well be' some services mentioned in the report which will not have gone on air, or will have been found assignments outside the 102.1-104MHz band, before the end of 1983. It seems reasonable to expect that, between 1 January 1982 and 31 December 1983, the sub-band 102.1-104MHz will be far from fully occupied by new BBC and IBA services in England. It may well not be occupied at all in Scotland, Wales and Northern Ireland, where pressures on the existing local radio sub-band are less heavy.

The HOLRWP report mentions that the use of the new frequencies above 100MHz will mean 'tuning beyond that part of the tuning scale where the existing network and local radio services are now to be found' (p24 para 5.17). We consider that this represents an ideal state of affairs in which to operate new assignments: listeners will have to make a conscious effort to tune to the new stations, and will be unlikely to hear any of the new services accidentally.

In the VHF context we support the option of a specific sub-band for community radio (HOLRWP report p38 para 7.15 (b)). This would mean that community stations might in the main cause interference only to each other. In view of the low power and limited geographical range of many of the new services, it is likely that a large number of small-scale stations, certainly sufficient to provide adequate evidence as to their viability in social and economic terms, could be accommodated within a relatively small sub-band.

In seeking an assignment for community radio pilot schemes, we also have to bear in mind the other type of community radio recognised by the HOLRWP report: the 'community of interest' stations.

Such stations would be likely to require higher power assignments than those aiming at more local neighbourhoods. Technically, the distinction between 'high' and 'low' power services may well be a gradual one, with stations of (say) 10w erp or less being decidedly in the latter category, and those over (say) 100w erp falling into the 'high power' category (erp = effective radiated power). High power assignments might be found in one of two ways: a) by bringing into service prior to the target date local service assignments planned for use by the BBC or IBA after the beginning of 1984 but before the implementation of the European VHF band-plan agreement in 1985. It is very wasteful of spectrum to have assignments waiting 'on the shelf' because their potential users are not ready, while there are other would-be broadcasters having to do without; b) by making temporary high-power assignments within the community radio sub-band. If the community sub-band were more than 600KHz wide, it would be possible for one high-power service to co-exist in any geographical area with a number of localised low-power services.

For this reason, and to provide adequate spectrum for all likely applicants, we propose that a sub-band 1MHz wide within the 102.1-104MHz allocation should be set aside during the years 1982 and 1983 exclusively for radio transmissions by organisations outside the control of the BBC and IBA. This sub-band might be divided into four channels, 200kHz apart and with 200kHz guard-bands between the extreme channels and the band edge. These channels can be organised in a self-managing system to provide a network of contiguous (if need be) local/neighbourhood services. If required a high-power assignment on one of the outer channels (1 or 4) could share a geographical area with low power local services operating on the other outer channel.

In view of the low power of the majority of proposed services, international interference is likely to occur only in an inward direction. In any event, international implications are likely to be no more problematic with this arrangement than with any other, particularly when the timescale involved is taken into account.

Medium and long wave Although we have suggested that the pilot scheme should operate on VHF, we are mindful of the fact that medium and long wave frequencies may in certain circumstances be of use to community radio interests.

Simulcasting (Simultaneous broadcasting on VHF and medium wave) We do not accept the arguments advanced in the HOLRWP report in favour of simulcasting. Over three-quarters of all households now have a VHF receiver, and the luxury of simulcasting is one which future services should be denied.

It is almost incredible that on the one hand lack of frequency space is advanced as an obstacle to the development of community radio while on the other hand BBC and IBA local services are permitted to use *two* frequencies for *one* service.

Licensing procedures for pilot community stations

(This is the text of Appendix II of the Community Radio Supporters' Open Letter to the Home Secretary.)

The Home Office should be responsible for licensing pilot community stations in the allocated sub-band, in accordance with the following criteria:

1. Prospective stations shall supply, at their own expense, a map outlining the proposed service area and a definition of the target audience. The target audience may be defined in one of two ways: a) as people who normally live and/or work within the geographical area defined as the service area; or b) as a specific minority which can be identified within a larger community enclosed by the target area. Such minorities might be disabled, religious or elderly interest groups, ethnic or racial groups, members of colleges, hospital patients, jazz or rock music fans, or any other factions whose needs are only sporadically catered for by our present broadcasting system.

2. Prospective stations should propose a) an operating frequency (this may be determined in consultation with any other community radio groups known to be operating or planning to operate in nearby areas), and b) an estimate of the power necessary to cover the target area outlined above, together with a description of the technical characteristics of the aerial system to be employed.

3. Stations shall provide documentary evidence of public support from within the target audience already identified for the new service: a suitable form in which this might be presented would be a petition signed by five per cent of the identified audience.

4. The onus shall be on the Home Office to demonstrate why a prospective service should *not* be given a licence rather than on the station to demonstrate why it should. This approach is a necessary precondition of a satisfactory pilot scheme. The only valid reasons for refusing a licence shall be a) failure to comply with the requirements set out above, or b) potential frequency congestion or interference on the proposed frequency. The Home Office shall be empowered to assign a station a frequency other than that originally suggested by the station, or to refuse to issue a licence under (b) above.

A frequency assignment is taken to have a two-dimensional nature, the first dimension being the frequency itself, the second consisting of allocation of broadcasting time. It would be perfectly possible for mutually agreeable stations to share frequencies between themselves, and to submit a joint application for a licence.

Financial status of stations Stations applying for experimental licences shall be assumed to be financially capable of sustaining the proposed service. Licences will be issued only to stations which are non-profit distributing. The licence application shall state the anticipated hours of transmission throughout the week. Stations which have not started transmitting the schedule of programmes proposed in the application document within three months of the date of issue of the licence shall be deemed to have withdrawn from any rights or obligations towards that part of the assignment not taken up.

Technical supervision Once a station's assignment has been taken up and the station is on the air, there is an adequate legal framework already in existence to take care of any interference caused by the transmissions. The local Post Office Radio Service can attend to any technical problems if and when they arise, and shall be empowered to close the station down in the case of persistent harmful interference.

Programming Stations shall have their programme content subject to the general laws of broadcast libel, etc. Stations shall be expected to come to their own arrangements with the Performing Rights Society, Mechanical Copyright Protection Society, Phonographic Performance Ltd., etc, and any other body with a legitimate interest in their programme content. Nothing in the licence shall exempt the station from its normal legal obligations. Advertising shall be permitted subject to the IBA Code of Practice.

Monopolies No one person, organisation or agents representing an organisation shall be permitted to exercise financial or editorial control over more than one station.

Public accountability The station manager, or a representative of the governing body of the station, shall make his or her name and address known to the public, and shall be responsible in the first instance for responding to any public criticism of the station's performance.

Bibliography

Anarchy 93, *Radio Freedom*, Freedom Press, November 1968

Aubrey, Crispin et al, *Here is the Other News*, Minority Press Group, 1980

Baron, Mike, *Independent Radio: The Story of Commercial Radio in the UK*, Terence Dalton, 1975

Briggs, Asa, *The History of Broadcasting in the UK*, Oxford University Press, 4 Vols., 1961, 1965, 1970, 1979

Gardiner, David, *Community Radio*, Undercurrents, 1971

Garnham, Nicholas, *Structures of Television*, British Film Institute, 1973, revised 1978

Heller, Caroline, *Broadcasting and Accountability*, British Film Institute, 1978

Lewis, Peter M., *Different Animals: Models of Structure and Finance in Community Radio*, International Institute of Communications, 1977

Lewis, Peter M., *Community Television and Cable in Britain*, British Film Institute, 1978

McCron, Robin, and Dungey, Jo, *Aycliffe Community Radio – A Research Evaluation*, University of Leicester, 1980

Partridge, Simon et al, *A Community Radio Station for the Hounslow Area: An Initial Feasibility Report and Some Guidelines*, Broadcasting Rights and Information Project, 1980

Turner, Nigel G., *Community Radio in Britain: A Practical Introduction*, Whole Earth Tools, 1973

Williams, Raymond, *Communications*, Penguin, 1970, revised 1975

Williams, Raymond, *Television: Technology and Cultural Form*, Fontana, 1974

GOVERNMENT REPORTS AND WHITE PAPERS ON BROADCASTING

Report of the Broadcasting Committee 1949, HMSO, Cmd. 8116, 1951

Report of the Committee on Broadcasting 1960, HMSO, Cmnd. 1753, 1962

Report of the Committee on the Future of Broadcasting 1974, HMSO, Cmnd. 6753, 1977

Tenth Report from the Select Committee on Nationalised Industries, Vol. I & II: Independent Broadcasting Authority, HMSO, 637-I/II, 1978

Observations by the Home Secretary and the IBA on the Tenth Report from the Select Committee on Nationalised Industries, HMSO, Cmnd. 7791, 1979

An Alternative Service of Radio Broadcasting, HMSO, Cmnd. 4636, 1971

Broadcasting, HMSO, Cmnd. 7294, 1978

Comedia Publishing Group
9 Poland St, London W1

Comedia Publishing produces books on all aspects of the media including: the press and publishing; TV, radio and film; and the impact of new communications technology.

The Comedia publishing series is based on contemporary research of relevance to media and communications studies courses, though it is also aimed at general readers, activists and specialists in the field.

The series is exceptional because it spans the media from the mainstream and commercial to the oppositional, radical and ephemeral.

No. 9.　**NUKESPEAK – The media and the bomb**
Edited by Crispin Aubrey
paperback £2.50 hardback £7.50

No. 8.　**NOT the BBC/IBA – The case for community radio**
by Simon Partridge
paperback £1.95 hardback £5.00

No. 7.　**PRINT – An industry in crisis**
by Frank Elston, Alan Marshall
paperback £2.25 hardback £7.50

No. 6.　**THE REPUBLIC OF LETTERS – Working class writing and local publishing**
edited by Dave Morley and Ken Worpole
paperback £2.95 hardback £8.50

No. 5.　**NEWS LTD – Why you can't read all about it**
by Brian Whitaker
paperback £3.25 hardback £9.50

No. 4.　**ROLLING OUR OWN – Women as printers, publishers and distributors**
by Eileen Cadman, Gail Chester, Agnes Pivot
paperback £2.25 hardback £7.50

No. 3.　**THE OTHER SECRET SERVICE – Press distribution and press censorship**
by Liz Cooper, Charles Landry, Dave Berry
paperback only £0.80

No. 2.　**WHERE IS THE OTHER NEWS – The news trade and the radical press**
by Dave Berry, Liz Cooper, Charles Landry
paperback £1.75 hardback £4.50

No. 1.　**HERE IS THE OTHER NEWS – Challenges to the local commercial press**
by Crispin Aubrey, Charles Landry, Dave Morley
paperback £1.75 hardback £3.50